The short guide to working with children and young people

Liesl Conradie and Tyrrell Golding

D0453261

First published in Great Britain in 2013 by

The Policy Press
University of Bristol
Fourth Floor
Beacon House
Queen's Road
Bristol BS8 1QU
UK
t: +44 (0)117 331 4054
f: +44 (0)117 331 4093
tpp-info@bristol.ac.uk
www.policypress.co.uk

North American office:
The Policy Press
c/o The University of Chicago Press
1427 East 60th Street
Chicago, IL 60637, USA
t: +1 773 702 7700
f: +1 773-702-9756
e:sales@press.uchicago.edu
www.press.uchicago.edu

British Library Cataloguing in Publication Data
A catalogue record for this book is available from the British Library.

Library of Congress Cataloging-in-Publication Data
A catalog record for this book has been requested.

ISBN 978 1 44730 023 6 paperback

Cover design by The Policy Press.
Front cover image kindly supplied by www.alamy.com
Printed and bound in Great Britain by Hobbs, Southampton.
The Policy Press uses environmentally responsible print partners.

FSC
www.fsc.org
MIX
Paper from
responsible sources
FSC® C020438

To Gustav and Alyssa (Liesl)

To Olivia (Tyrrell)

Contents

List of tables and figures

Tables

Figures

Acknowledgements

Acknowledgements for the poem on p 78 and the pen pictures:

Leonie Campbell	Sarah Horn
Dawn Dixon	Lysette Shaw
Emma Farmer	Tamara Smith
Lisa Fuller	Nicola Southgate
Alison Gray	Reece Wells
Tracey Hennighan	Sasha Wells

We would like to thank all the young people, colleagues and students, past, present and future, who have supported, engaged in and informed our work and this book. Last but not least, we would like to thank our friends and families for their unending encouragement, support and patience.

List of abbreviations

BASW	British Association of Social Workers
CACHE	Council for Awards in Care, Health and Education
CRB	Criminal Records Bureau
CV	curriculum vitae
ECHR	European Court of Human Rights
EPPE	Effective Provision of Pre-school Education
EU	European Union
EWO	education welfare officer
EYFS	Early Years Foundation Stage
GCSE	General Certificate of Secondary Education
GSCC	General Social Care Council
ITT	initial teacher training
LGBT	lesbian, gay, bisexual and transgender
NEET	not in education, employment or training
NSPCC	National Society for the Prevention of Cruelty to Children
NVQ	National Vocational Qualification
PGCE	Post Graduate Certificate in Education
PSHE	personal, social and health education
QTS	qualified teacher status
SCITT	school-centred initial teacher training
UK	United Kingdom
UN	United Nations
UNCRC	United Nations *Convention on the Rights of the Child*
US	United States
YMCA	Young Men's Christian Association
YOT	Youth Offending Team

Glossary

Ableism is the act of discriminating or being prejudiced against people with physical impairments or learning disabilities.

Accommodation is part of Piaget's work on cognitive development. In order for a child to understand new information they have to alter their current ideas in order to accommodate the new information.

Accountability is a very important notion and means that organisations and individuals must explain and take responsibility for their actions and the subsequent results.

Adolescence is the stage in a person's life when they are developing from being a child into being an adult. It is a process that is characterised by change and can be a very challenging time for young people (and those around them).

Ageism is the unfair treatment of someone based on their age. Young people are often treated in a way that would be unacceptable for other groups, for example you often see signs on shop doors saying 'only two school children at one time'. You would not expect to see a sign saying 'only two disabled people at one time'.

Agent refers to someone who can make things happen.

Aims are broad or general statements of what you would like to achieve.

Animism is the tendency to give life-like qualities to non-living things.

Anonymity means not sharing someone's name. If you keep a reflective diary or write documents at work, you may be expected to anonymise your papers by using fake names, for example.

Anti-discriminatory practice is a way of working that aims to challenge and diminish the causes and impact of **discrimination**.

Anti-oppressive practice is a way of working that aims to reduce the structural, personal and cultural systems that create oppression.

Assimilation is part of Piaget's theory of cognitive development and refers to the adaptation process that takes place when we are introduced to new ideas or experiences: instead of changing completely to accommodate the information into our ideas and schemas, we subjectively modify the information in order to fit in with our already existing ideas and schemas.

Association is a term used most often by youth workers. It aims to highlight the importance of young people having a space to go to 'hang out' with their peers and some key professionals as well as to learn and engage with activities.

Attachment theory is the theory that concerns the attachment between one person and another.

An **au pair** is a young person who normally comes from a different country in order to help with childcare and housework in exchange for pocket money, food and board.

Bilingual means the ability to speak two languages. A bilingual person may not necessarily be as competent in both languages.

Biological construction is the notion that, for example, gender is a biological or natural occurrence. You can see the gender of someone; it is therefore determined by nature rather than made by humankind (socially constructed).

Black and minority ethnic (BME) is a term used to describe people from minority groups. Minority groups within the UK consist of people who would not describe themselves as 'White British'.

Boundaries determine the limits that you can go to. It gives a dividing line that should not be crossed. This dividing line separates the personal from the professional.

Budget deficit refers to a situation where there is more money going out of, for example, government coffers than money going in. There is therefore a shortage of money to cover all expenditure.

A **child** is often seen as a boy or a girl who is not yet an adult, that is, up until the age of 18. However, practitioners now identify that there is a stage, referred to adolescence or youth, which precedes adulthood. This period is now studied specifically on Child and Adolescent or Youth Studies courses and specialist services are now considered for this group. While there may be some differences across professionalisms, it is usually considered appropriate, unless you are their parent, to call someone a child until they attend secondary school and then they should be referred to as a young person.

Child protection processes and policies in the UK are supported by the Children Act 1989 and 2004. These Acts place the welfare of children at the heart of matters that affect them and put a statutory duty on adults working with children to report suspected child abuse. Child protection is more often referred to under the wider concept of 'safeguarding', which also includes guidance on the prevention of child abuse and cruelty. One of the ways that organisations are expected to work in a preventative manner is by working together and sharing information where appropriate.

Childcare is care provided to a child by the government, an organisation or a person, normally when the parents are not there.

A **childminder** looks after one or more children and normally is self-employed and owns their own childminding business or works with/ for another childminder. They usually work from their own home.

Class/es. British society is traditionally separated into class/es. Your class is defined by your socioeconomic status, which of course can change over your lifetime.

Class oppression is any type of discrimination, oppression or prejudice against someone as a result of their class.

A **community centre** is a venue that is used as a central meeting place within a community. It can be used for cultural, social or leisure and sport activities. It is also normally a popular site for children's groups and activities and youth groups.

The **concrete operational stage** is the third of the four stages of cognitive development as set out in Piaget's theory of cognitive development. It normally takes place between the ages of seven and 11. During this stage, children are able to think logically about concrete events.

Connexions was originally set up as an advice and guidance service for young people aged 13 to 19 (and up to 25 for those with particular needs). Where the service still exists it may be one of two things: in some areas it continues to be an information, advice and support service whereas in other areas it is an umbrella service operating as the outward face of integrated youth support services.

Conservation is the ability to remember what stays the same in an object that, for example, changes shape and what stays the same. According to Piaget, this ability develops in the **concrete operational stage**, which takes place during the ages of seven and 11.

Constructionism means that something is made or constructed either biologically, for example gender, or socially by how the members of a society or community view for example children and their role in society.

Continuous Professional Development (CPD) is a term used to describe the ongoing training and development activities that professionals undertake throughout their career. These learning activities can be either formal, such as short courses, or informal, such as taking part in collaborative working activities. Whatever form these activities take, it is important that they meet the ethos of CPD, which is to maintain and develop an individual's competence in their practice throughout their career.

A **continuum** is something that is continuous. It is often used to describe or define a range of ideas or things that are related or at different points on the same scale such as a political belief, which can range from right-wing to left-wing.

Critical theory stems from Marxist thought and was developed by the Frankfurt school of social thinking in sociology. At its most basic it holds that all of society and life must be investigated and critically looked at. Critique and investigation are central to critical theory.

Culture(s) is the term we use to describe the customs, beliefs and way of life of a group of people. So we might compare youth culture in the 1960s with that of the youth culture in the 1980s in the UK.

The **curriculum** is the range of subjects that are studied in schools such as geography, English and mathematics (that is, the national curriculum). Youth work also has a curriculum, which aims to cover the subjects needed to support young people in their emotional and social development, such as healthy eating and cultural awareness.

A day-care provider is a childcare provider that looks after children during the day. It can also involve medical day care and leisure activities for children of all ages. Day care is also a popular option for older people and also for disabled individuals of all ages.

Demographic refers to certain characteristics of populations, for example race, gender and income level.

According to the UK's Equality Act 2010, a person has a **disability** if 'they have a physical or mental impairment' and 'the impairment has a substantial and long-term adverse effect on their ability to perform normal day-to-day activities' (YouGov, 2011). In other words, they have an illness, injury or condition that means that they find it difficult or can't do things that people without a disability can do. This could mean that they can't do everyday things such as eating, washing, shopping or walking.

Disadvantaged is used to describe someone who does not have all the resources or the right situation to have an equal or similar position to others in society.

Discrimination happens when a person or group of people are treated differently from others. It is generally accepted that there are two kinds of discrimination. The first is **negative discrimination** where a group is treated badly or less favourably, maybe because of their gender, the colour of their skin or their sexuality. The other is **positive discrimination**, which is the process of giving an advantage to certain groups who are often negatively discriminated against. This might be to increase the number of women in the workplace.

Diversity is used to describe variety. It is most often used to describe ethnic or cultural diversity, where there are people from a number of different cultures or ethnic backgrounds living in the UK.

Early childhood is a stage in human development. It ranges from birth up to the age before starting mandatory education. This may be from birth to five years of age or in some countries birth to seven years of age.

Early school is Erikson's third stage of the psychosocial development model and ranges from the ages of three to five. The crisis or issue that needs to be overcome during this stage is that of initiative versus guilt.

Early years is a separate life and development stage. It also encompasses the various approaches to working with infants, toddlers and children from birth to the age of five/seven.

Ego development outcome refers to a state where the ego (built on Freud's id, ego and superego) is able to develop in order to reach the next stage in Erikson's psychosocial development theory. During each stage, a person encounters a conflict or crisis that needs to be resolved. Depending on how the stage is handled, this can lead to a positive or negative developmental **outcome**. For example, during infancy the outcome will be to be able to trust people or not.

To **empower** someone is to give someone the authority, responsibility or freedom to do something. Professionals often try to **empower** children and young people to make the decisions that affect their lives.

Equal opportunities is the policy, that is, the best course of action, for ensuring that all people within a particular setting are treated equally and have the same opportunities.

Equality can be defined as the state of being equal. In terms of work with children and young people it can also be used to define and describe the personal value and professional ethic that states that all people, no matter what their religion, race, ability, age, gender, class or sexuality, should be treated equally.

Equilibrium refers to a balanced state, where opposing ideas, influences and situations are worked out in order to give a clear and balanced state within the mind.

Ethics are the accepted beliefs about what is right or wrong in any given situation. Ethics may be defined by a culture or community, or by the values of a profession.

A person defines their **ethnicity** based on belonging to a certain groups of peoples who have a common culture or tradition. Someone who is perceived to belong to an minority ethnic group belongs to a smaller ethnic group than the dominant one in any society. However, it is important to note that someone who belongs to an 'ethnic minority' in one country may belong to the dominant group in another.

Evaluation enables you to assess the quality, impact or importance of something. For example, a youth worker might evaluate a session that they have delivered to a group of young people or a teacher might evaluate how many students in their class have understood an aspect of a lesson.

Every Child Matters is a range of documents that underpinned a New Labour government agenda, which was in part brought about by the tragic death of Victoria Climbié. The term Every Child Matters refers to these documents as well as being the title of a Green Paper published in September 2003 (Hoyle, 2008). All of this was made legal by the Children Act 2004.

Experiential learning is learning that is based on experience.

Field is the term used by professionals when they are discussing people who work or practise in a profession. It *does not* mean that you work in a field; unless you are a detached worker maybe, but that is a different thing! The opposite of working in the field is to be an academic who writes about a subject rather than being a **practitioner**.

Fine motor control refers to the skill of using the smaller muscle groups in order to complete tasks that are precise. For example, it is involved when your finger picks up a raisin.

Formal education refers to more formal ways of learning, usually in a classroom or lecture hall. It is often seen as the opposite to **informal education**.

Formal operational stage is the last stage in Piaget's stages of cognitive development. It starts at age 12 and lasts into adulthood. According to Piaget, during this stage, children are able to start thinking abstractly, in other words thinking about thinking and things such as religion and love.

Gender is the term we use to describe the socially constructed notions and characteristics attributed to men and women. They are the ideals that we have regarding what it is to be masculine and feminine. This is different to sex, which refers to the biological and physiological characteristics that 'define' men and women.

Grammar schools are one of the types of schools in England and Northern Ireland. They are selective, that is, they take only the cleverest of pupils as opposed to comprehensive schools, which take all the pupils in their area. The pupils will be offered a placed based on their results of an entrance examination or the 11 Plus.

Group work is the process of working with two or more young people. The groups can be formed for a range of different reasons. They might be based around geography, such as a village youth club; specific interests such as girls groups; or around learning, for example the Duke of Edinburgh's awards schemes or babysitting courses.

Heterosexism is a viewpoint that assumes that everyone is heterosexual. It may be evidenced by a worker who automatically assumes that a young man will be attracted to young women and so jokes with him about not having a girlfriend yet.

HIV/AIDS AIDS stands for acquired immune deficiency syndrome and it is an infectious disease caused by the human immunodeficiency virus (*HIV*). A person will therefore first test HIV positive and this will eventually lead to AIDS. This is a serious disease that leads to death and has a major impact on societies and public health.

Holistic refers to looking at the whole person or situation, not just at parts of it. The whole person include their physical and mental states as well as the social environment.

Holocaust refers to the genocide of six million European Jews during the Second World War. The Nazi German government during this time systematically murdered approximately one third of the Jewish people living in Nazi-occupied territories. Various other groups were also systematically murdered by this government, including homosexuals, Romani and disabled people.

Homophobia is the fear of people who are gay, lesbian, bisexual or transgender.

Hypothesis is a proposal or statement that you make, which you want to try to find out if it is true or not.

A person's **identity** is made up of their personal qualities. The factors that affect this include the person's age, **race**, **culture**, religion, **gender**, whether they have a **disability** and so on. It refers to how we see ourselves in relation to other people.

A person's **ideology** is their beliefs or ideals. A person, group or organisation can have an ideological perspective on any matter, but it is referred most often to a political or economic stance. For example, the political parties in England were traditionally separated into very different ideological stances: Labour was associated with the working classes and the Conservatives were associated with business. Their political policies are informed by their ideologies and outline what they think should be done for the good of society.

Implementation refers to the act of putting a plan into action and carrying out what you have decided to do.

Inclusion refers to the ideals that underpin good practice around discrimination and oppression. Practitioners aim to include people from groups who have been traditionally 'excluded' due to their ability, age, **gender**, **race**, religion and so on.

Industrial Revolution is the time period characterised by rapid industrial development.

An **infant** is a very young baby – roughly up to the age of one year.

Informal education is often seen as the 'opposite' of formal education but should be seen as being complimentary to it.

Institutional racism refers to organisations (or institutions) such as the police or schools, whose structures and principles create a culture of racism. Rather than oppressing the individual it has the opportunity to oppress the majority of the people within the group being discriminated against.

International Labour Organization (ILO) is a United Nations agency that has as its main aim to support labour (workers). It formulates international labour standards about, for example, working conditions,

Latency is another term used to describe the school-age child (aged six to 12 years) stage of Erikson's stages of psychosocial development.

Life stage transition refers to a period or process of change from one stage or situation to the next, for example changing from primary to middle or secondary school.

Marxism was devised by Karl Marx and Friedrich Engels. It is an ideology that believes that the state exploits the masses. Class struggle is a central tenet of Marxism.

Methods are what you do in order to complete a task.

Middle school refers to the three-tier system where an extra school is built in between primary school and secondary school.

A **nanny** is someone whose role it is to care for children. This can be one or more children within a family or a nanny-share with another family. A nanny is a paid employee of the family.

Nursery school caters for children between the ages of three and five years. It is an educational establishment that cares for children as well as educates them. Nursery schools are independent and separate from primary schools. Nursery schools must be registered and must also be inspected by the government's regulatory body.

Object permanence means that a child is able to realise that an object continues to exist even though they can't see it.

Objectives refer to how you are going to achieve the aims that you set. They refer to the methods or activities that you will be involved in to achieve your aims.

Ofsted is the Office for Standards in Education, Children's Services and Skills. It is impartial and also independent, and reports directly to parliament. Ofsted inspects settings in order to ensure that children, young people, families and learners receive the best possible care, education and skills.

Oppression is the unfair treatment or domination of people that prevents them from having the same opportunities and freedom as other sections of society.

An **outcome** is how we measure the result of an intervention or piece of work with children and young people. This may be a 'hard' outcome such as the number of GCSEs achieved or a 'soft' outcome such as learning to participate in a group.

Peer is a term used to describe someone who is of the same age or group, but not necessarily a friend.

A **policy** is guidance or instructions of what to do in a given situation. It is usually written down after being agreed by relevant people. It includes codes of conduct and recruitment policy. It can also be made by the government or a political party, such as its policy on immigration or health. There are also less formal policies that you might come across within a team regarding, for example, who makes the tea – in some places administrative staff do this whereas in others you make a cup if you fancy it and offer to make one for everyone else. These policies are more informal and reflect the culture of the team and the way that it operates.

Positivist refers to the perspective that social scientists should use quantitative methods to find out (research) aspects in the social world. Facts and figures are important for positivists.

Play work is essentially a career; however, it is also the activity of the play work practitioner. It aims to enhance children's lives and learning through play.

Practice refers to what we actually do in our work with children and young people.

A **practitioner** is someone who works in a job that requires specific skills. Therefore, we would argue, that everyone who works with children and young people is a practitioner, even if they are not professionally qualified.

Pre-operational phase is the second stage in Piaget's stages of cognitive development. It ranges from the ages of two to seven years.

Preschool – see **nursery school**

Private sector is the part of the economy of the country that is not owned or controlled by the government. Organisations within the private sector are set up to make their owners and shareholders money.

Professional can be used in a number of ways. It can be used to mean anyone who is working with children and young people because they are paid, although often these individuals are referred to as **practitioners**. More often though it is used to refer to people who have a specific professional qualification, for example in early years, social work or youth work.

Universities approve and certify their own courses. However, any degree which also gives the students graduating a professional qualification, such as those in social work and youth work, must also be approved by the relevant **Professional, Statutory and Regulatory Body (PSRB)**. This will probably mean that the course may have specific requirements that the PSRB demands, such as a certain number of days of assessed practice, and the level and type of qualification of any supervisor needed.

Psychological refers to aspects that can impact on the mental or emotional health of a person and start in the mind.

Psychosocial refers to the psychological and social aspects that influence personality and behaviour from birth onwards.

Puberty refers to the stage in a human's physiological development when they become capable of sexual reproduction. It is the stage when bodily changes take place and sexual maturation is reached in order to allow for reproductive functioning in both sexes.

Public sector is the part of the country owned and run by the government. It includes local authorities, some schools and police services.

'Race' is a contested term with no scientific basis, but is used to refer to a group of people with the same characteristics, that is, skin colour or shared history and culture, for example the British.

Racism is the belief that people's personal characteristics or abilities are affected by their race. If you are racist, you think and behave negatively towards people whose race is different from your own.

Reflection is the process of thinking about an event or action, either currently or in the past, and considering how it went. There are a number of models that practitioners use to inform their reflection.

A **reflective** practitioner uses a reflective cycle or model to think about an event or action, how it went, why it went that way and what they need to do differently or the same next time a similar situation occurs.

Reflexive is something that happens automatically without conscious control, for example a knee-jerk reaction.

Resilience refers to the ability to recover quickly from setbacks.

From a youth work perspective, **residentials** are trips or visits which involve groups staying away overnight. This might be for one night or many. The term **residence** refers to where people live or reside and so this term will mean different things to social workers, for example, who may be involved with decisions regarding where children and young people should live.

Safeguarding is broader than child protection and refers to the efforts made to protect children from ill-treatment, as well as preventing children's health or development being negatively impacted on and ensuring that all children are growing up in safe and secure environments.

Safer working practices refer to the ways that work is done in an organisation in a safe way. In an organisation working with children and young people, aspects such as criminal record checks and appropriate relationships and behaviour with children and young people are needed as well as appropriate training.

Schemas refer to the categories of knowledge and ideas that we have that help us to understand and interpret the world and what happens in it. Our experiences will add to or change our already existing schemas about the world.

School age refers to the age range of children who would normally be attending school within a particular country. School age can therefore differ from country to country.

A **school refuser** is a child or young person who refuses to attend school. The reasons for this could be that 'the child or young person has a *phobic reaction* either to the general school situation or to a particular situation or thing within the school' or that they have 'a fear of attending school but the main source of the worry is leaving home or separating from family' (www.handsonscotland.co.uk/topics/anxiety/school_refusal.html).

Sector – see **private sector, public sector** and **third sector**.

Sensorimotor stage of cognitive development is the stage in Piaget's stages of cognitive development that ranges from birth to the age of two.

Services user is the term used to refer to the people who use services provided by certain professionals.

Sexism is the belief that members of one sex, usually women, are less able or intelligent than another. This can promote sexist stereotypes such as women being worse drivers or that they are better suited to certain job roles.

Sexual orientation refers to whether you are physically attracted to people of the same sex as you or not. Therefore your sexual orientation could be bisexual, gay, lesbian or heterosexual.

Social construction refers to the notion that certain aspects in social life are made by humans and can change based on what people want to belief, think and the ways they want to act.

Social exclusion is what can happen when people do not feel part of the society in which they live. This could be due to poverty, unemployment or the way they feel that society sees them (for example when young people from a certain estate, school or culture are always spoken about in the media in a negative way). It is the opposite of **social inclusion**.

Social inclusion is the process of trying to minimise or diminish the effects of social exclusion.

Social work is the range of services provided by the local authority, through social services departments, to help and support people who are more vulnerable, for example as a result of age or illness.

A **social worker** is a professional who provides help and support to individuals who need it. They may work for a private organisation or a local authority.

Special educational needs has a legal definition set out within the Education Act 1996. It states that a child has a special educational need if they have a learning difficulty, which means that special provision in education must be made for them.

Sure Start children's centre is defined within the Child Care Act 2006. It refers to a place or a group of places that are run by or on behalf of a local authority and that provide a first port of call for would-be parents, parents and further family members on all matters to do with early childhood support and care. This includes healthcare services, information support and activities.

Symbolic function is the first substage in Piaget's second stage of cognitive development, the preoperational stage. This normally takes place between the ages of two and four. Toddlers can think about objects even though they might not be real or present. Pretend play features heavily at this age, for example playing in a play kitchen 'making' cups of tea.

The **third sector**, also known as the voluntary and community sector, covers all other areas not covered or run by the state (government) in the public sector, or the private sector. It is a term that only started to be used during New Labour's (1997–2010) time in government in the UK.

A **transition** is a change from one thing to another. For example, adolescence is the transition everyone goes through as they develop from a child into an adult.

Union can refer to many different things, but in a work context it often refers to trades unions, which have been shortened to just union. It is an organisation that works to protect the rights, including pay and working conditions, of people within a particular industry.

Values are the ideas that you have about what is important or not or what is good or bad. You will have both personal and professional values, which may not always align perfectly. What is important is that your personal values do not affect your professional judgements.

Variables are things that can change.

Vertical transition refers to transitions and changes, that is, movement from one life stage to another, and indicates a change of status, for example from primary school child to secondary school child. Horizontal transition is less dramatic – it refers to the movements made on an everyday basis, for example from home to school.

Vocation is a type of job that you feel that you need to do and you feel particularly suited to. Professions in areas such as education, health and working with children and young people are often considered to be vocational.

Voluntary engagement is a key value specifically within youth work where young people should be able to voluntarily choose to engage with youth services. The other side to this is that young people must be equally free to choose not to engage with youth services if they do not wish to.

Voluntary Ofsted Childcare Register is for service providers for children and young people who do not have to register on the Ofsted Childcare register but that voluntarily choose to do this. This can include nannies, childcare for children over the age of eight, activity-based settings and also short-term care.

Vulnerable people are more at risk than other members of society, whether this is physically, emotionally or mentally. They may be at risk of or vulnerable to being hurt, influenced or attacked by other people.

Welfare state is an expression used to describe a government that introduces a tax in order to provide social services such as healthcare and unemployment benefit to people who need them.

Working class can be a contentious term but in general it refers to people who work for someone else for wages, especially in a manual labour role.

Work–life balance in short refers to having enough time to work but also enough time to do other things outside of work.

Young people refers to an age range of usually 11 to 19 years old rather than a life stage such as adolescence. The term highlights the importance of 'people' rather than children and acknowledges young people's rights in order to empower them. It is generally used by professionals such as youth workers.

Youth work is a particular form of work with young people rather than a generic term for any work with young people. It is informed by a specific set of values perhaps most notably that young people voluntarily engage with youth workers. For more information on youth work, go to: www.nya.org.uk

Zone of proximal development is the difference between what a child can learn by themselves compared to what they can learn if someone with more knowledge helps them.

1

introduction to working with children and young people

In this first chapter of *The short guide to working with children and young people* we will give you a brief overview of why work with **children** and **young people** is needed. We will introduce you to the nature of working with children and young people, including identifying the different age groups that **professionals** work with; for example you may already be asking yourself when does a **child** become a young person? We will also begin to identify the different professionals who work with children and young people, perhaps challenging some of your assumptions. For example, youth workers are not a type of social worker. All the aspects of working with children and young people that we introduce you to in this chapter we will develop further in later chapters.

How to use this book

This book is intended to be a concise presentation of the key factors and facets that professionals face. We have written this book hoping that it will be clear and understandable to anyone who picks it up and flicks through the pages. However, we have specifically tried to make it useful and applicable to readers who may wish to enter the working with children and young people **field**, whether they are a young person researching and planning for their future career or someone ready to retrain and face fresh challenges. This book might also be one of the first books you are introduced to in your studies after you have made a decision to work with children and young people.

Whoever you are, we recognise that there is a dizzying array of professionals working in the **sector**. We hope that by reading this book and undertaking some of the activities we suggest, you will find your path to the right future career.

All the way through the book you will find key words and phrases within the text in **bold**. You will find a plain, user-friendly definition of these key terms in the glossary on pages ix to xxvi. We have tried to ensure that this glossary is easy to understand and includes all the key terms used by **practitioners** who work with children and young people, including some terms not referred to directly by us. In fact, we feel that this is almost a chapter in its own right. This is because a key aspect of becoming part of a community of practice (Wenger, 1999) is understanding and adopting the language used by the practitioners and professionals within it. We hope that we have written in a style that is easy to read and follow, but we have not 'dumbed down' in our identification of the concepts to include. We suggest that you keep your own record of any words or phrases that you do not recognise when you first come across them in the course of your wider reading or research.

Pause for thought and reflection

Throughout this short guide to working with children and young people, we will include brief activities in each of the chapters. These will usually be an opportunity for you to pause and reflect on the topic or theme being discussed. These activities are not compulsory and will not prevent you from continuing with your reading and understanding of the chapter. However, if you are using this book to support you to consider a possible future career working with children and young people, these activities will guide you through the process. The activities will also aid you to make sense of the theories covered and introduce you to the idea of putting theory into practice (using theory in real situations).

Pen pictures

In some of the chapters we will also be using pen pictures. A pen picture is a way of trying to create a picture with words instead of a drawing. In this book we will be using pen pictures of some of the main practitioners who work with children and young people. Hopefully, these will give you some good examples of real working situations, which we have drawn from our own experiences and the experiences of colleagues.

Reflective journal

Most students studying to work with children and young people are advised to keep a reflective journal. This might also be called a reflective diary, learning journal or practice recording, but it often involves students undertaking similar processes.

Reflect: to think carefully, especially about possibilities and opinions. (Cambridge Dictionaries Online, 2011)

The purpose of keeping a diary or log of your reflections is to enable you to identify your thoughts and feelings about things that you read, theories that you come across or something that happens while at work. There is really no right or wrong when it comes to what to write about. However, as a general guide, we suggest that if there is something that you find yourself thinking about after work or a theory or news item you read or hear about really makes you think or feel something, it might be worth writing about it.

Reflection, especially with regard to practitioners working with children and young people, has been written about a lot. This is because, essentially, reflection is a process that aims to support us to think about things that have happened and identify what we can learn from these events. For example, if I pick up a hot pan from the cooker and burn my hand, I may reflect on this and realise that I should use a tea towel or wait for the pan to cool. If I don't think about the event at all, I may not identify the cause and effect between the hot pan and my burnt hand and I might make the same mistake again. It is important to also reflect on things that go well to ensure that you can try to replicate them. If you are interested in learning more about reflective practice then we suggest that you do an online search. Alternatively, we have included some key texts on various topics in the 'Further reading' section at the end of each chapter.

While we will introduce a different reflective model in Chapter Five, a particular favourite model of the authors of this book was produced by Gibbs (1988). His model is of particular interest for us as he identifies the role of feelings in our evaluation and interpretation of a situation (see Figure 1.1).

Figure 1.1: Gibbs' reflective cycle

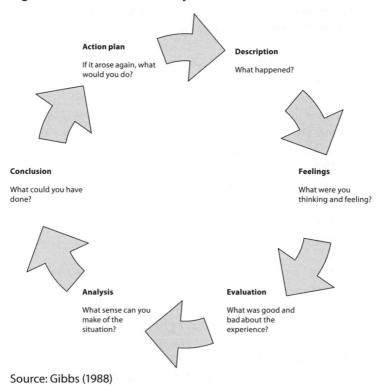

Action plan

If it arose again, what would you do?

Description

What happened?

Conclusion

What could you have done?

Feelings

What were you thinking and feeling?

Analysis

What sense can you make of the situation?

Evaluation

What was good and bad about the experience?

Source: Gibbs (1988)

Gibbs' (1988) reflective cycle provides us with a structure for our reflection and provides prompts for us to think through the facets of an issue or event. Starting at description, you can address each question, writing as little or as much as you think relevant to the topic of your reflections. Whether you choose to write this process up or not, you can use it to think through most things. For example, you could employ it as usefully to think through a meeting at work as you could to support a young person to think through an argument with a friend.

One of the most important points on the cycle is the point at which you action plan. For reflection to be a useful process you need to think about what will change and what you can do next. Without this aspect, nothing will change. It is the difference between a circle and a cycle: a circle goes round and round, staying on the same course in the same space; a cycle is more like a spiral, which has a similar pattern but moves forward at the end of each rotation.

Pen picture – Lucy

Lucy was a new youth worker. She was having trouble building a positive relationship with a group of young men in an evening youth club. As part of the course she was studying she had to keep a learning journal. Using Gibbs' (1988) model as a structure for her journal, she started to work through the issue. She identified that as she was 21 years old and the young men were 16 to 17 years old, she felt that she didn't present herself as a confident member of staff and the young people took advantage of her being so near their age.

Completing the process she identified an action plan for her next session. She decided on leading a part of the session to support the young people to look at the youth club rules on behaviour again. She felt that this would give her a role while allowing her to address the issues around the young people's behaviour towards her.

After the session, Lucy completed another learning journal entry. She described the session and completed each aspect of Gibbs' cycle. Again she identified an action plan for her next session with the young men, which was to continue to build on the good practice she had now started.

In the pen picture above you can see Lucy using a reflective cycle to develop her work. She is also using a theory to inform her practice. As Lewin (1951, p 169) is famous for saying, 'there is nothing more practical than a good theory'.

If you do decide to undertake any of the '*pause for thought and reflection*' activities, we suggest that you make notes in your reflective journal. You can make your notes in any form that works for you, for example on a notes app on your smart phone, on loose paper or on a dedicated notepad, or you could set up a pro forma based on one of the reflective models you have found. However you choose to reflect on the key themes within this book or the interesting things that occur to you, we suggest that you think about how you look after these recordings. It's important that if you are writing about your personal feelings, you take care who might be able to see what you write. You should also protect the **anonymity** of any colleague, child or young person you might be referring to. We suggest you could do this by giving the individuals false names.

Further reading and online resources

We appreciate that this is a *short* introduction to working with children and young people. Not only is the topic of children and young people a huge one, when you also add to that the varied professionals who work with them at any given stage, you begin to realise what an enormous topic this is. At the end of each chapter we have included further reading and online resources related to the relevant topic or theme addressed for you to find out more if you wish.

Who is this book for?

Primarily, this book is for people living in the United Kingdom (UK), which is made up of England, Scotland, Wales and Northern Ireland. We hope that it will be useful and interesting to anyone already working, either in a paid or voluntary capacity, with children and young people and those interested in developing a career in the field.

Wherever possible we will give examples of and signpost you to useful online resources and books that cover the entire British Isles, which covers the UK, all of Ireland, the Channel Islands and the Isle of Man (Directgov, 2011a). We will also bring in relevant information from other countries to give you a broader, more international perspective on working with children and young people where relevant.

What is working with children and young people?

The authors of this book have worked with children and young people in a range of settings throughout their careers. These include **playwork**, community work, holiday schemes, sport, international projects, schools and **residentials**, to name a few! One thing that we have both been faced with is the challenge and attitudes of adults who do not work in the sector: 'Work with young people? I couldn't do that! What a nightmare! You must have the patience of a saint!' While we have paraphrased a career's worth of responses, the essence is the same and after all our years of working we still can't disagree with these comments more. This is because during all our years of **practice** and as a result of our professional training, we have observed and learnt some key things that we will support you to think about throughout this book:

■ Working with children and young people is a privilege, not a right.
■ Children and young people need you to be their youth worker, teacher or social worker and so on, *not* their friend or parent.

- Except in specialist circumstances, children and young people do not need to be 'saved'; often they are the best people to resolve their own issues.
- You will probably learn more from working with this group than they will, especially at the beginning.
- Working with these groups can be *very* challenging but we have never found any other job so rewarding.

As you will see in the following chapters, working with children and young people takes a range of important skills, has particular challenges and there is a range of different professions and perspectives. It is not the intention of this book to present a definitive perspective on each area of practice. Rather, we intend to introduce you to the key areas or practice, perspectives and roles in order that you can develop your understanding and begin to identify the areas of work that you might be interested in.

These different professions have different professional identities, some focus on specific age groups while some focus on the way they engage or work with children and/or young people. One of the aims of this book is to support you to understand different professions as well as understanding the **values** and **ethics** that underpin their practices.

Pause for thought and reflection

Please read the following poem. Try to think about or reflect on what it might mean for people who work with children and young people. If you are planning on keeping a reflective journal, write down your thoughts and feelings.

Children live what they learn

If a child lives with criticism, He learns to condemn.
If a child lives with hostility, He learns to fight.
If a child lives with ridicule, He learns to be shy.
If a child lives with shame, He learns to feel guilty.
If a child lives with tolerance, He learns to be patient.
If a child lives with encouragement, He learns confidence.
If a child lives with praise, He learns to appreciate.
If a child lives with fairness, He learns justice.
If a child lives with security, He learns to have faith.
If a child lives with approval, He learns to like himself.
If a child lives with acceptance and friendship, He learns to find love in the world. (Anon)

Why work with children and young people is needed

Work with children and young people is required for a variety of reasons. Some of these reasons are inherent to the issues that children and young people face; we will discuss these in Chapters Six, Seven and Eight. Other reasons are due to the importance that broader society attaches to children and young people. We will be addressing the social construction of childhood and youth in Chapter Three. Before we move on to that though we are going to look at the rationale for working with children and young people in this section.

Type of work

There are many ways in which you can work with children and young people. As you will see throughout this book, many of these roles can be found along a **continuum**. In Chapter Eight we will discuss the informal/formal education continuum, but you can also find practitioners working across a continuum of compulsory/voluntary engagement. This could also be used to describe the education continuum, but also includes other practitioners.

You will find practitioners working with children and young people wherever they are at, both geographically and developmentally (child and adolescent development will be explored more fully in Chapter Four). Therefore you will find professionals who work specifically with an age group, such as playworkers, **early years** workers or youth workers. These workers may support children and young people in a general sense or more specifically to address issues that are relevant to their age and situation, such as developing social skills at an early age or the challenges of managing and maintaining **peer** relationships as children grow into young people and through to adulthood. We will be looking at these careers in greater detail in Chapters Six, Seven and Eight. As you can see from Table 1.1, some of these practitioners work with more than one age group. We have only looked at each profession once with regard to the age range most relevant to their work or most appropriate for this book. It is important to note that some professionals, such as social workers, may work across or with various age ranges, including adults. If you are interested in a particular type of work we suggest that you use the resources we suggest to do further research into that career.

Alternatively, you will find professionals who have expertise in a certain area such as housing or health that, through the course of their working week, might support and engage with children and/or young people as part of their role.

Role undertaken

Within the varied professions, you may undertake a range of different roles depending on the group or individual you are working with and the situation they are facing. At any point you may be an advocate, leader, role model, teacher or educator, safeguarder or facilitator. Understanding the differences between these roles and how they can be utilised to **empower** and support children and young people is part of the professional training process. As part of this process you may discover that there is no absolute right and wrong in most situations. What we can assure you is that for most of the professions a key part of your training will be undertaking work-based or placement learning. As such, learning from your mistakes will form an important part of your studies and also your future career development.

Table 1.1: Practitioners divided by age group

0 –5 years	5–12 years	13 –19 years	All
Au pair	Child psychologist	Careers/Connexions advisor	Community development
Childminder	Au pair		Community organiser
Early years Foundation Stage Advisor	Education psychologists	Education psychologists	Health professionals
Nanny	Education welfare officers	Education welfare officers	Housing professionals
Nursery sssistant	Learning support assistant or advisor	Learning support assistant or advisor	Police
Nursery nurse	Parent Support Advisor (PSA)	Young people's worker	PCSOs
Nursery teacher	Playworker	Youth worker	Social work
Preschool assistant	SEN coordinator practitioners/ counsellors	SEN coordinator practitioners/ counsellors	
Play group worker	Teaching	Teaching	
Sure Start worker	Youth justice worker	Youth justice worker	

Please note: this is not an exhaustive list of all practitioners who may work with children and young people. It highlights some of the main practitioners working in this area. You may also find that the titles of these practitioners change over time and so you should use this table as a starting point.

Your motivation

When deciding on a career working with children and/or young people, a key consideration is your own motivation. If you are thinking of a career in this field as a knee-jerk reaction to something that you have seen on television or read in a newspaper or feel that someone needs to 'save' the children or young people shown on the television or written about in the newspaper, you may wish to reconsider. Being a professional in this field requires you to adhere to clearly set **boundaries** and ethics. This is something that we will explore further in Chapter Five.

Role modelling

> No printed word, nor spoken plea can teach young minds what they should be. Not all the books on all the shelves – but what the teachers are themselves. (Rudyard Kipling)

Role models are important for all children and young people. They find their role models in a range of people such as their close family and friends as well as the significant adults in their lives such as teachers or famous people. Without appropriate role models, children and young people are susceptible to less positive influences. As Ingram and Harris (2001, p 19, emphasis added) state:

> (Professionals) act as **Role Models** so young people can learn:
> Caring and being cared for
> Disagreeing and remaining friends
> Negotiation and compromise
> Building relationships that are open, honest and based in trust.

Whatever role/s you may have in the future, if you are working with children and young people you will need to consider how you adopt your position as a role model. As we stated at the beginning of this chapter, we consider working with children and young people a privilege and so we do not see being a role model as an inconvenience. We see this role as an important tool through which we can build relationships and develop learning opportunities.

Pause for thought and reflection

Please consider the following questions. We suggest that you jot down your answers somewhere as they will be useful and interesting to reflect on in the future (perhaps when you have finished reading this book or when you are applying to study a relevant course).

- Which age group do you think you would like to work with?
- Why do you want to work with this age group?
- Are you already aware of anyone who works with children and young people in this age group? If so, what is it that they do?
- Are any of the professions that you are already aware of, including those in Table 1.1, of interest to you as a future profession? If so, why?
- What experience do you already have of working with this age group?

As you learn about working with children and young people through reading this book and wider research, your answers to these questions might change. This is good! Not only is being adaptable and open an important skill for those who work with children and young people, but you will also be able to see how reading the book and researching more widely has impacted and informed your views. This will be useful to discuss if you choose to apply to a university or college to study a course or apply for a job in the field.

Requirements for working with children and young people

If you are currently working with children and young people, you will have had to successfully complete some kind of background check. In England and Wales this is known as the Criminal Records Bureau (CRB) check. Alternatively, in Scotland you will need a Disclosure Scotland certificate (also known as a Disclosure) and in Northern Ireland you will need a Protection of Children and Vulnerable Adults check. This is because you are working with a **vulnerable** group.

There are other requirements that you will become aware of when you enter the field. For example, people who work with children and young people in the UK are expected to undertake training and consider their **continuous professional development**. As part of the training available to you there may be local training, perhaps provided by your organisation or a local training agency. There may also be nationally validated certificates in your area of work. These are usually validated by awarding bodies such as City & Guilds or the National Open College Network.

If you wish to take your career further still, many occupations have professional status, such as teaching, **social work** and **youth work**. Professional qualifications for these can be gained through completing a BA Honours degree or above. For those occupations where there is a professional qualification, you may find that it is essential to gain it in order to work in that role. However, for many of the roles, you can develop your career by undertaking courses as you work and through volunteering. In Part Two we will be identifying some of these professions. At the end of each chapter there will be links to useful websites where you can find out more about the career and training options for each.

Generally, for each career path there will be a **professional, statutory and regulatory body** that impacts on the work of practitioners within the field. Where there are degree courses or national certificates, such as Youth Work (the professional qualification route for youth workers) and Working with Young People (the certificate for youth support workers), there will be a professional, statutory and regulatory body that informs what should be taught in these programmes and the skills that practitioners need at each level, in the case of young people the National Youth Agency.

Studying for a degree that awards you a professional qualification can be seen as more challenging than completing a purely theoretical degree such as childhood studies or youth studies. This is usually because the work-based or placement aspects can be seen to add extra stress. However, you should consider this carefully. One perspective on this is that working with children and young people takes particular skills and these are not purely academic. Throughout our careers we have met students who could write a first-class academic essay on how to build relationships with children and young people but who could not maintain a conversation with a real young person. Of course, we have also met students who had great interpersonal skills but struggled academically. Studying a course that is work based or has placements allows you to evidence to future employers the tangible skills that you have gained. You can add the experiences to your curriculum vitae (CV) and will have real experiences to support you in job interviews. You may also be able to get paid while you learn.

The other side of the argument is that you would be better off successfully completing a purely theoretical degree than dropping out of a work-based course if it is too much for you. You can also supplement your academic study with part-time or voluntary work with children and young people during the holidays. This might also be useful for you if you are not yet sure which profession you want to eventually go into. However, you need to be aware that if you decide that you want to go into social work, for example, you will need to either apply to do another degree to qualify or study for a Master's degree in social work.

Whichever route you think might be for you, we suggest that you take some time to work with different age groups, in different job roles, to ensure that you know which profession is right for you. You might also want to talk to professionals who are currently working and carefully explore the different course options available. We would also suggest that you consider carefully whether you could spend some time volunteering with children and young people in a range of settings. There are some professional courses for which 'relevant vocational experience' is a requirement. It will also give you the opportunity to try different roles as part of your ongoing research into the field. While you may feel that you don't have the time to volunteer or you just want to get on with your career, the voluntary work may lead into employment as you gain experience, skills and contacts. In this field, at least to begin with, you may have to 'speculate to accumulate'.

Pause for thought

At this early stage, we wonder whether a particular profession, area or age group has struck you as particularly interesting in terms of a future career. We suggest that you take a few minutes to write down your thoughts and feelings at this point.

You might also wish to consider what kind of training or qualifications you will need in order to work in this area. How do you like to learn? Can you envision yourself studying at university? More importantly, can you envision yourself at your graduation having successfully completed your studies? Perhaps you would like to be in work while you gain your qualification. There are many possible ways in which you can achieve your goals, but at this point it will be useful for you to identify your hopes for your professional future. These early thoughts, feelings and goals will then inform your reading of this book.

You may also feel that you do not know enough about the different professions who work with children and young people. That's fine! We will be looking at this in much more detail in Part Two. You might also feel that you need some more experience working in the relevant area before you commit to the profession and perhaps three or more years of study.

The policy context of practice

So far we have identified and discussed what working with children and young people is all about. We have briefly challenged you to think about why work with children and young people is needed and the nature of that work. Before we move on to the next chapter of this book, we would like to briefly highlight the impact of **policy** on our practice.

It is important to note that the current policy context of your country or region can and will have an impact on your practice as a professional. So too will the nature of the organisation you work in. You may have a certain view of where and how each of the professions works; for example, social workers are employed by the council, teachers wear suits and teach at the front of a classroom and youth workers wear hoodies and play pool. As you will see as you continue through the chapters, we hope to challenge these notions.

Throughout your career you are likely to find that change is the only constant. The regular review of professional values and standards by your professional, statutory and regulatory body will ensure that your work is still meeting the demands of employers and the people you work with. Changes in government through the normal election process, now every five years, will see different political parties, with their different political agendas, come to power and therefore may identify different priorities for your work. Finally, throughout your career you may work for different organisations and may be in different sectors, and you will need to place your practice within these different elements, as you can see in Figure 1.2.

While this book is not solely aimed at those of you who live in England, a good example of the impact of changes in policy at a national level on professional practice at a personal level is the overnight impact of the

Figure 1.2: Placing your practice within a policy, professional and organisational context

policy changes between New Labour (**welfare state**) and the coalition government, constituted of the Conservative and Liberal Democrat Parties (localism/Big Society). The agenda can be seen to have shifted fundamentally from being 'top down' as established by the New Labour government, to being driven by locally established agendas, delivered at a local level, which the coalition government has established.

A change in government, and therefore government agenda, will impact on who identifies the work priorities of professionals in the field, including which groups should be targeted and how need is defined. This particular change in agenda has had a profound impact on funding streams, priorities and indicators and is a topic that we will return to at relevant points throughout the book. We will continue to look at the relevant national and international policies relating to work with children and young people in Chapter Two.

We hope that whatever your motivations for reading this book, you enjoy the process and find the information that you are looking for. We also hope that this book is useful and the beginning of a journey of knowledge gathering: 'The most important attitude that can be formed is that of the desire to go on learning' (Dewey, 1938, p 49). Whichever profession, if any, you may be interested in or are progressing towards, you will need to be committed to continuing your learning, something that we will look at in greater detail in Chapter Five.

SUMMARY OF KEY POINTS

In this chapter we have started to explore the following ideas:

■ Working with children and young people requires specific skills, professional values and personal commitment.
■ Each professional group, such as social workers or teachers, works differently.
■ Children and young people have differing needs to adults/older people.
■ Reflection is an important tool for those working with children and young people to help them to identify what they can learn from events.
■ There is a range of professional bodies that regulate the different careers.
■ Professionals work within a national and organisational policy context.

FURTHER READING

A book that looks comprehensively at reflective practice, which will support you as you start to engage with this type of practice, as a student through to professional practice (there is also a companion website to the book): Bolton, G. (2010) *Reflective practice* (3rd edn), London: Sage Publications.

Donald Schon is one of the key writers on reflective practice. Why not read the original source for yourself?: Schon, D. (1991) *The reflective practitioner: How professionals think in action*, San Francisco, CA: Jossey-Bass.

A book offering a collection of chapters by a range of different authors, covering a variety of the important topics in an easy and accessible manner: Zwozdial-Myers, P. (ed) (2007) *Childhood and youth studies*, Exeter: Learning Matters.

ONLINE RESOURCES

Department of Education (2011) *Children and young people*, www.education.gov.uk/childrenandyoungpeople

HM Government (2011) *Number 10: The official site of the Prime Minister's Office*, www.number10.gov.uk/

InfEd (2011) *The informal education encyclopaedia*, www.infed.org

Northern Ireland Direct (2011) *Department of education*, www.deni.gov.uk/index.htm

Scottish Government (2011) *Education and training*, www.scotland.gov.uk/Topics/Education

Welsh Government (2011) *Careers with children and young* people, http://wales.gov.uk/topics/childrenyoungpeople/working/careers/?lang=en

2

national and international policy for childhood and youth

For many people who go into a career that sees them working with children and young people, they usually do so visualising the children and young people themselves. They may visualise themselves helping a young person complete a maths puzzle that they wouldn't have been able to achieve before. Or they may dream of coaching a group of young sportsmen and women to win a competition.

In this chapter, we are going to ask you to think beyond the work that happens directly with the children and young people. We are going to ask you to think about the wider possible implications of the work. We are also going to ask you to consider what factors might inform the professional actions of someone working with these groups. As you do so, you might want to reflect back on the figure we looked at in Chapter One, which placed practice within a policy, professional and organisational context (Figure 1.2 on p 18).

Reflective activity

A child or young person is sitting in a school corridor. They are crying as once again they have been bullied. As they sit there they try to think of a way to stop the bullying: hide, hurt themselves or just refuse to go to school. An adult walking by notices the child or young person. They stop, ask them what the matter is and work with them to stop the bullying.

Think about this example and consider the following questions:

- What is the impact on the child or young person?
- What is the impact on their friends?
- What is the effect on their family?
- What is the effect on their community?
- What is the effect on their country?

As we move through this chapter, we would like you to think about the broader impact of work with children and young people. The result of supporting a child or young person can have a ripple effect that impacts throughout our society. However, it may also have an impact on the child, potentially for the rest of their lives. This reflects the values underpinning one line of the poem we read in Chapter One: 'If a child lives with acceptance and friendship, He learns to find love in the world' (anon). We will look at this notion again in more detail in Chapter Nine, where we consider a model by Thompson (2006), which identifies the importance of personal, social and cultural influences on our values.

As we move through the present chapter, we will outline the development of national policy as it relates to working with children and young people in the UK. Before we start though, we think that it is important to briefly outline the international political agenda. This is because, as you will see, some international policies have informed the development of policies in the UK.

We are then going to briefly look at some of the key historical policies that have informed work with children and young people. However, most of this chapter will be focused on the key policy changes that were introduced by the New Labour government in the UK from 1997 to 2010. Finally, we will conclude the chapter with a look at the policies introduced by the Conservative and Liberal Democrat coalition government since it came to power in May 2010.

Before we start, we feel that we should introduce the different terms that we will use in this chapter: Act, convention, guidance, legislation and policy. First, an 'Act' refers to an 'Act of Parliament' and it creates a new law. For a number of different reasons, the government may wish to change or amend an Act or repeal it (cancel it) if it is no longer applicable. The term 'legislation' refers to an Act or the law. A 'convention', in this particular use of the term, is used to describe 'legal agreements made by governments ... [and] are part of international law, and not just advice to governments' (Kapell, 2010, p 6). 'Guidance' is just that, guidelines on how one should behave in certain situations, rather than how one must behave. Finally, a 'policy' is a bit like a guideline, that is, it suggests the best course of action rather than creates a law that forces or forbids an action. A policy can be applied at the national, organisational and personal levels and is usually put into place using procedures.

The international political and policy arena and its impact

There are various potential pitfalls that we might find ourselves plummeting towards if we are not careful. The first is that we talk about policy, that is, 'the way we do things round here' from our national perspective and expect or assume that it is true or the same all over the UK. This is just not the case and throughout this book we have been careful to try to signpost you to the correct information. Wherever you are sitting reading this book, it is important that you take ownership of your own learning journey. You will need to check things as they stand in your country, especially given the rate of change we have seen worldwide since the 2008 global financial crisis. At an international level, there has been the 'Arab Spring' and the fall of Colonel Gaddafi. At a European level, there is the European debt crisis (*The Wall Street Journal*, 2011) and in the UK there have been changes in government. These have prompted ideological and political shifts. While these changes have appeared to be unusually fast paced, change is an inevitable part of working with children and young people. Whichever profession you might wish to enter, you will need to gain the skill of ensuring that you keep up to date with these changes. However, before you can do that you need to ensure that you have some awareness of what has gone before or what underpins the current situation.

While it is not the remit of this chapter or indeed this book to equip you with an in-depth knowledge of the policies that relate to children and young people across the globe, there are a couple of key international political and policy perspectives on children and young people that inform our national perspectives and so it is important that we identify them before moving forward.

International

One of the fundamental **ideologies** that underpin our national relationship with the international community is a commitment to protecting and promoting human rights. While our struggle for human rights can be traced back to the earliest times of civilisation (Franklin and Eleanor Roosevelt Institute, 2001), it was the founding of the United Nations (UN) that has informed modern practices.

Founded in 1945, directly after the Second World War, the UN was originally established by '51 countries committed to maintaining international peace and security, developing friendly relations among nations and promoting social progress, better living standards and human rights' (UN, nd).

Purpose of the UN

The UN has four main purposes:

- ◼ 'to keep peace throughout the world;
- ◼ to develop friendly relations among nations;
- ◼ to help nations work together to improve the lives of poor people, to conquer hunger, disease and illiteracy, and to encourage respect for each other's rights and freedoms;

■ to be a centre for harmonizing the actions of nations to achieve these goals' (UN, nd).

The Universal Declaration of Human Rights was ratified on 10 December 1948 (UN, 1948). In its 30 articles it establishes what the UN believes to be fundamental truths such as 'all human beings are born with equal and inalienable rights and fundamental freedoms'.

The events of the Second World War, particularly the **holocaust** and associated war crimes, had a huge impact on the formation of the UN and other initiatives. If you are unaware of the main events of this key period in modern history, we strongly suggest that you find a way to learn more. You will find that you have a much greater understanding of the reasoning behind the development of the organisations and treaties identified in this chapter if you do.

Another key international document is the United Nations *Convention on the Rights of the Child* (UN, 1989), which is commonly known as the UNCRC or just CRC. The convention addresses the specific and particular needs of children, which it defines as anyone under the age of 18. There are 54 articles in the convention and two optional protocols. The articles include statements such as article 2, which stresses that any country that has adopted the UNCRC must 'respect and ensure the rights (of) each child ... without discrimination of any kind, irrespective of the child's or his or her parent's or legal guardian's race, colour, sex, language, religion, political or other opinion, national, ethnic or social origin, property, disability, birth or other status' (UNCRC, 1989). UNICEF, which was set up in 1946, states that 'the Convention on the Rights of the Child is the most widely and rapidly accepted human rights treaty in history' (UNICEF, 2012). There are four core principles or ideas that underpin the UNCRC, as you will see in the following box.

UNCRC core principles

The four core principles of the convention are:

- non-discrimination;
- devotion to the best interests of the child;
- the right to life, survival and development;
- respect for the views of the child (UN, 1989).

Europe

The European Convention on Human Rights (Council of Europe, 1953) is a Europe-wide treaty established to protect the human rights and fundamental freedoms of the citizens of European countries. One of the incentives for the development of this convention was the events of the Second World War across Europe. Another was as a reaction to the Universal Declaration of Human Rights identified above.

The convention was written by the Council of Europe, not to be confused with the European Union (EU). Founded in 1949, the Council of Europe is an organisation that consists of the 47 countries of Europe. It was established to promote democracy and human rights across all countries situated in the geographical zone of Europe. The UK and Ireland are founding members of the Council of Europe.

The EU, on the other hand, currently has 27 members 'that have delegated some of their sovereignty so that decisions on specific matters of joint interest can be made democratically at European level' (Council of Europe, 2011). Again, both the UK and Ireland are members of the EU, but only Ireland is a member of the Eurozone. This is the name given to the 17 member states of the EU that use the same currency: the Euro.

You may have heard of the European Court of Human Rights (ECHR), which is the court that enforces *The European Convention on Human Rights*. It is 'housed' in Strasbourg, France, which is also the home of the European Parliament. Commonly, we hear about the ECHR in a negative light. Some national newspapers in the UK accuse the ECHR of meddling in Britain's decision-making process, for example demanding that the government gives prisoners the right to vote, which they don't currently have. On the other hand, the ECHR has also challenged the government when it has planned to deport people to countries where they may face torture or unfair trials. Anyone who thinks that their rights, as set out in the European Convention on Human Rights, have been violated by their government, can take their case to the ECHR. This means that there is an independent body that can arbitrate been the individual and a government.

Key historical national perspectives

For the purposes of this section, we are going to separate policy history into three distinct periods of time as they relate to work with children and young people:

- prior to William Beveridge's key report of 1942;
- from 1942 to the period of Conservative government (1979–97), including discussing the impact of the Albemarle Report (1960);
- the period of New Labour (1997–2010), leading into the new Conservative/Liberal Democrat coalition government.

Policy before Beveridge, pre-1942

You could write a timeline for each nation in the UK and Ireland featuring the key policies and events that relate to children and young people, perhaps starting with the Magna Carta in England and Wales in 1215, the Great Charter of Ireland in 1216 and the 1265 establishment of the Scottish Parliament (Marsh, 2007). However, we are not going to start from this point or go into such detail, but hopefully this illustrates what a challenge it is to highlight some of the key incidents across these five nations over an almost 800-year history!

Prior to the establishment of the welfare state in 1945, much of the services we now associate with this term were provided by local authorities, voluntary organisations and the church (Field, 2010a). Some see the establishment of the Young Men's Christian Association (YMCA) in 1844 as being the first dedicated youth organisation (Smith, 2002) and it is often cited as being the beginning of youth work as we might define it today. We think that the time at which some legal aspects of work with children and young people were introduced might surprise you. For example, prior to the Elementary Education Act 1870, most schools were administered by the church, **grammar schools** were often funded by wealthy merchants, and individuals made their living by teaching the three 'R's – reading, writing and arithmetic (Parliament UK, nd). The Elementary Education Act 1870 was the first Act in Britain that specifically dealt with education and it was passed in order to develop schools in places where there weren't any. A similar Act was passed in Scotland in 1872 – the Education (Scotland) Act (Parliament UK, nd). However, it was not until 1880 that another Act made education compulsory for 5- to 10-year-olds, which was in response to issues around children working – the Education Act 1880. By 1899, the age of compulsory attendance had risen to 12 years old, although truancy was a problem due to families still being dependent on their children's incomes. These early 'ragged schools' were as much a part of the origins of youth work and **informal education** (Smith, 2001) as they were more 'formal' education. It was also during this period that 'youth' as a specific and discreet age was identified and that the notion of 'adolescence' as a life stage was developed by psychologists, such as G. Stanley Hall (Smith, 2002).

Policy relating to young people's rights in the UK date back to the 14th century (1300s), although at that time they were not the kind of 'rights' that we would recognise today. Most of the policy relating to children and young people throughout this period and into the late 19th century (1800s) was in regard to their control and punishment or their education, as we have seen above. It was only in 1904 that the UK government introduced the Prevention of Cruelty to Children Act. This gave the National Society for the Prevention of Cruelty to Children (NSPCC) a statutory right to intervene in **child protection** cases. It is still the only non-governmental body with the statutory authority to take children into care.

Alongside developments in educational policy during this period were changes in the way children and young people were seen with respect to the law. The Children and Young Persons Acts of 1932 and 1933 extended the role and remit of juvenile courts and introduced supervision orders and probation respectively. It was only in 1932 that capital punishment, that is, the age at which you could be hanged, was raised to 18 and the age of criminal responsibility was raised from seven to eight years old. It also brought together current child protection legislation, including notions of neglect, and the employment of *school-age* children under one Act. These issues will be explored further in Chapter Three.

Beveridge and beyond: 1942 onwards

The *Report of the Inter-Departmental Committee on Social Insurance and Allied Services* (Beveridge, 1942) is more commonly known as the Beveridge Report, after William Beveridge who chaired the committee that published it. It is often identified by authors on the subject as being a key milestone in the history of UK social policy. This is because the report was a very influential document in the establishment of the welfare state. Beveridge identified five 'giant evils' in society: squalor, ignorance, want, idleness and disease and the report established the reform needed to address these. In fact these five evils were directly related to five pillars of the welfare state (Alcock, 1996):

■ Squalor ⇨ social housing provided by the state
■ Ignorance ⇨ education provided by the state
■ Want ⇨ introduction of the social security system
■ Idleness ⇨ commitment to full employment
■ Disease ⇨ National Health Service.

As part of the **implementation** of the ideals in the Beveridge Report, the National Insurance Act 1946, the National Health Service Act

1946 and the Pensions (Increase) Act 1947 were introduced. Other key pieces of legislation throughout this period included the Education Act 1944, which among other things raised the school leaving age to 15 years and made free school meals compulsory.

A key publication for youth workers was the Albemarle Report (Ministry of Education, 1960). Perhaps in response to, among other things, the post-Second World War baby boom, the report was synonymous with a 'golden age in youth work' and 'famously declared that the primary aims of the youth service should be association, training and challenge' (Smith, 2002). Throughout the 1970s, 1980s and 1990s, major policy decisions tended to be more related to education, justice and social work, until the arrival of the New Labour government in 1997. The key Acts introduced in this period include the Children Act 1972, which raised the school leaving age to 16, and the Children Act 1989, which aimed to ensure that commitments under the UNCRC were met.

Other key events during this period include the age at which someone was perceived to be an adult being reduced to 18 in 1970 and the introduction of the Gillick competency in 1985. This is the right of a child under the age of 16 to give informed consent, without a parent, when they are deemed to be sufficiently 'mature'.

New policies introduced by New Labour

In 1997, a New Labour government was elected to power. The UK had been governed by the Conservative Party since 1979 and so it might be said to be the beginning of a new ideological perspective in government. It was definitely a period of great change for those who worked with children and young people, with the rate of new policies and initiatives being introduced referred to as a 'tsunami' (Davies, 2009, p 188) by some.

When New Labour came to power, the political objectives around 'youth policy' could be distilled into four themes:

- active citizenship (rights & responsibilities);
- lifelong learning (education, education, education);
- **social inclusion** (a hand up, not a hand out);
- community safety (tough on crime, tough on the causes of crime) (Williamson, cited in Harrison et al, 2007, p 34).

There were a number of significant national policies and legislation introduced in this period. Depending on where you lived in the British Isles, there were some differences, for example *Every child matters* (HM Treasury, 2003) was relevant only in England, not in Scotland, Wales or Northern Ireland.

The main policies, Acts and guidance introduced were:

- the Children Acts 1989 and 2004;
- the introduction of tuition fees (1998);
- the National Minimum Wage Act 1998;
- Sure Start (1998);
- *Every child matters* (HM Treasury, 2003);
- *Youth matters* (DfES, 2005a);
- *Youth matters: Next steps* (DfES, 2006);
- *Working together to safeguard children: A guide to inter-agency working to safeguard and promote the welfare of children* (DCSF, 2006, 2010);
- *Aiming high for young people: A ten-year strategy for positive activities* (DCSF, 2007);
- *Guidance for safer working practice for adults working with children and young people* (DCSF, 2009).

Every child matters (2003), as stated above, was relevant only to England as were many of the other Acts at this time, so you could in fact argue that only every child in England was perceived to matter. While it is often presented as being solely brought about by the murder of Victoria Climbié by her aunt and her aunt's partner in 2000, it is important to note that it also built on existing plans to strengthen preventative services (Hoyle, 2008) and the government's commitment to the UNCRC in 1991. There were five **outcomes** associated with the

Every Child Matters agenda. These were the government's aims that every child, no matter what their background or circumstances, should have the opportunity to:

■ be healthy;
■ stay safe;
■ enjoy and achieve;
■ make a positive contribution;
■ achieve economic well-being.

The Children Act 2004 was the legislation that underpinned the changes needed, including establishing a new role of children's commissioner. In reality, the term 'Every Child Matters' actually refers to two things (Hoyle, 2008). The first of these is the Green Paper that was published in 2003, which became the Children Act 2004. The second is a series of publications that was published by the government in 2005 in order to support local authorities in implementing their duties outlined in the Children Act 2004. This had such a fundamental impact on the way the services for children and young people work together that we have dedicated the next section of this chapter to it.

Reflective activity

Think about what informs work with children and young people. You might like to come back to aspects of this as you work through this book.

What are the government's priorities? Education is your starter for 10. Why does the government think it's important?

At a local level, who does your local authority/district council or parish council employ or work with to provide services for children and young people?

As an individual, why do you want to work with children and/ or young people?

You might like to think about how these different aspects of policy, practice and preference come together to inform your thinking about work with children and young people.

From 'silos' to 'integrated working'

While the death of Victoria Climbié may have been a key catalyst for change in policy, there was a political drive towards working in a more integrated way for some time. However, while there has been the impetus and legislation for working together, there is no definitive model for how different professionals and organisations should work together. Rather, there are a range of models that can be employed depending on the situation, organisations involved and the outcome needed.

The change in working practices for professionals that was introduced during the New Labour years involved moving from 'silo working' (where professionals worked in their own specialist teams) (see Figure 2.1) to 'integrated teams' (where a range of professionals from different perspectives work together in the same team). In the context of a silo way of working, a child or young person and their families worked with one service at a time. Potentially, this meant that they could get to the end of a waiting list for one service to be referred to another service and be stuck on another waiting list. The alternative **method** proposed during the New Labour years and continued today is, as mentioned, an integrated method of working (see Figure 2.2). Now members of these different services are 'integrated' into multidisciplinary teams. Children, young people and families can now access these services in one place and this enables team members to appropriately evaluate and meet the needs of children, young people and families.

There are two main strengths of this change in working practices for professionals. The first of these is that it provides a 'one-stop shop' for children, young people and their families so that, as mentioned, they can engage with one service and be able to access a range of professionals and thus the team is 'wrapped around' the child/young

Figure 2.1: A representation of silo working

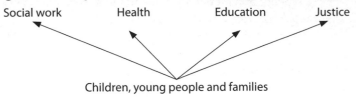

Children, young people and families

Figure 2.2: A representation of 'integrated working'

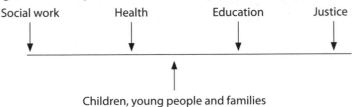

Children, young people and families

person. The second is that this change in practice hopefully develops a more **holistic** 'diagnosis' of the child or young person's needs rather than the agency approach as exemplified in Table 2.1.

Working together

This process of integrated or multidisciplinary working usually occurs where all those services are provided by one organisation such as a local authority. Where this can't or doesn't happen, professionals/organisations might work in 'partnership'. This is a term often used generically when people work together but there are distinct ways of working in partnership.

Payne (2000) identifies four different terms that relate to working together: coordination, collaboration, teamwork and partnership. Initially, they may appear the same, but there are some subtle differences. When agencies work together to ensure that their services do not compete with each other and there is no duplication of provision, this would be referred to as 'coordination', whereas

Table 2.1: Agency responses to the same presenting problem – aggression

Juvenile justice	Social services	Education	Psychiatry
Referral to police: decision to charge	Referral to social services	Referral to education department	Referral to child psychiatrist
⇩	⇩	⇩	⇩
Pre-sentence report completed	Social work assessment conducted	Educational psychology assessment	Psychiatric assessment
⇩	⇩	⇩	⇩
Sentenced to custody	Decision to accommodate	Placed in residential school	Admitted to regional inpatient unit
⇩	⇩	⇩	⇩
Labelled as a young offender	Labelled as beyond parental control	Labelled as having a learning difficulty	Labelled as having a mental health problem

Source: After Malek (1993, cited in Walker, 2003, p 78)

'collaboration' is the process of agencies working together, which may lead to coordination. The collaboration of colleagues within the same work group, whether they come from the same or different professions, is referred to as 'teamwork'. Finally, 'partnership' is a term used when organisations are collaborating over a long period of time. If there are joint funding bids or responsibilities involved, a partnership agreement might be written to clarify each organisation's roles and responsibilities. This term is also used to describe how professionals work with their client group, for example the way in which social workers engage with parents, which is set out in the Children Act 1989.

Why collaborate?

The New Labour government established the need for local authorities to promote integrated working in the Children Act 2004, which included a duty to cooperate. In order to ensure that *all* services for children and young people in an area were involved in the coordination process, children's trusts and the Compact were established.

Children's Trusts 'are the sum total of cooperation arrangements and partnerships between local organisations with a role in improving outcomes for children and young people' (Every Child Matters, 2010). The Compact is an agreement between the government and the **third sector**, now more commonly known as the voluntary and community sector. It is a kind of partnership agreement that aims to develop better working relationships between the government and the voluntary and community sector in order to achieve mutual or collaborative advantage.

Collaborative advantage

Collaborative advantage will be achieved when an objective is met no organisation could have produced on its own and when each organisation is able to achieve its own objectives better than it could alone. (Huxham and Vangen, 2005, cited in NCVO, 2007)

While the focus appears to be on local collaboration, organisations can work collaboratively at a strategic, regional or national level. This will be informed by the kind of work being undertaken, the nature and objectives of the organisations contemplating collaboration and the period over which the collaboration will be undertaken (NCVO, 2007).

Voluntary and community organisations can collaborate in a number of different ways. The main way in which organisations do this is to work jointly to deliver a service or project. You might find a large organisation with skills and capacity supporting or engaging with smaller organisations, such as a national organisation developing and providing training and resources that are used by smaller organisations. If needed, organisations collaborate to create a brand new organisation in order to meet a need that the partners are currently unable to accomplish. Another form, epitomised by the YMCA structure in the UK, is 'where a "parent" organisation governs a group of "subsidiary" organisations' (NCVO, 2007, p 1). Alternatively, maybe due to an overlap of organisational objectives or due to funding constraints, organisations may merge to create one new organisation. An example of this is No Smoking Day and the British Heart Foundation, which merged in 2011 due to No Smoking Day losing all of its government funding (Williams, 2011).

Virtually any kind of work can be done collaboratively depending on what is required by the different organisations involved. As stated previously, organisations might work together to provide a service or to campaign for change in policy or legislation. Another way in which groups work collaboratively is to share office space (and the costs involved) or support functions such as payroll or purchasing. Working collaboratively is underpinned by the notion that it will enable the groups involved to increase their efficiency and to achieve something that they cannot do alone.

However, working collaboratively isn't always the answer. If organisations rush into working together without considering whether they are suited to working together or whether the piece of work in question is the right one to collaborate on, it is unlikely to have a successful outcome. It can be a challenging and stressful process that does not guarantee success. However, if planned well and thought through, it can be a hugely beneficial way of working.

The future

Without being able to see into the future, we cannot tell you exactly what will happen. However, if the coalition government introduces half as many policies as the New Labour government, we are likely to be facing a period of great change. Given that cuts in spending in all areas of public life have been announced in order to reduce the national deficit and the announcements ministers have made thus far, we can see that professionals working in this field will need to be able to manage, keep up to date with and cope with change.

We will identify some of the most relevant policy changes and initiatives brought about by the coalition government in the appropriate chapters in Part Two of this book. However, some of the broader 'highlights' are:

- the scrapping of ContactPoint, the online database of information about all children and young people in England under the age of 18;
- the launch of the 'Big Society', including the introduction of the National Citizenship Scheme for young people aged 16 years old;
- the expansion of the academies system with the Academies Act 2010 and the introduction of the Free Schools Programme;
- the introduction of the pupil premium, to aid schools in the support of children and young people from low-income families and those in care;
- a new tuition regime for university fees in England.

As we stated at the beginning of this chapter, we have identified just some of the key policies that relate to work with children and young people. Other authors may have chosen to identify different ones and, depending on which nation you are working in, some may be more important than others.

Our aim in this chapter is not to equip you with all the information regarding every relevant policy but to support you to see how international and national policies affect the work of professionals on a day-to-day basis. We hope that you will now see the importance and impact of policy on work in this area and that it may have whetted your appetite to find out more about social policy.

SUMMARY OF KEY POINTS

In this chapter we have:

- identified and explored why it is so important that adults working with children and young people understand the policies that relate to their work;
- identified the main international and national policies that relate to children and young people, particularly their rights;
- seen how policies in the UK have developed over time and made note of the very swift introduction of policy into the field since 1997;
- explored how the changes in policies have directly informed changes in working practices.

FURTHER READING

The following two documents offer an insightful look at youth work policy specifically; however, they are also relevant because of their European approach:

Verschelden, G., Coussee, F., Van de Walle, T. and Williamson, H. (2009) *The history of youth work in Europe: Relevance for youth policy today*, Strasbourg, France: Council of Europe Publishing (also available as a PDF from http://youth-partnership-eu.coe.int/youth-partnership/documents/Publications/Others/History_of_youth_work.pdf).

Verschelden, G., Coussee, F., Van de Walle, T. and Williamson, H. (2010) *The history of youth work in Europe: Relevance for youth policy today: Volume 2*, Strasbourg, France: Council of Europe Publishing (also available as a PDF from http://youth-partnership-eu.coe.int/youth-partnership/documents/EKCYP/Youth_Policy/docs/Youth_Work/Research/YK_Youth_Work_Vol_2.pdf).

An edited text that brings together chapters from a range of authors in two sections: theory and practice; and policy and practice. It is not an entry-level text, but it will support you to develop your understanding of these aspects of our work: Wood, J. and Hine. J. (eds) (2009) *Work with young people: Theory and policy for practice*, London: Sage Publications.

ONLINE RESOURCES

The following are some key websites that we hope will start you off in your search for policies relevant to the country in which you work.

England: Department for Education: www.education.gov.uk

Wales: The Welsh Government: http://wales.gov.uk/topics/ childrenyoungpeople/

Scotland: The Scottish Government: www.scotland.gov.uk/Topics/ People/Young-People

Northern Ireland: Office of the First Minister and Deputy First Minister: www.ofmdfmni.gov.uk/index/equality/children-young-people.htm

Ireland: Department of Children and Youth Affairs: www.dcya.gov.ie/ viewdoc.asp?DocID=120

Europe: European Union—Council of Europe Youth Partnership: http:// youth-partnership-eu.coe.int/youth-partnership/index.html

3

social construction of childhood and youth

This chapter will introduce the idea that all over the world there are children but that not all children have a 'childhood'. Childhood is not a universal state enjoyed by all children in the world. And so we will explore the question, what is childhood? Normally if you ask someone this, the answer will refer to a child's age and an explanation of a time that people grow and develop until they reach biological or physical maturity and adulthood. This is the biological perspective on being a child and progressing through youth to adulthood. This developmental stage approach is advocated by some biologists and psychologists, for example Piaget and Erikson (we will learn more about these and other theorists in Chapter Four). However, there is another way to look at the time of childhood and youth. This is known as the **social construction** of childhood. In this chapter we will briefly explore the biological as well as the social construction of childhood.

The biological construction of childhood

As noted above, the **biological construction** of childhood refers to the time that children grow and develop until they reach biological maturity and is confined within a specific age range. This way of understanding childhood is endorsed by the United Nations *Convention on the Rights of the Child* (UNCRC) (UN, 1989), which we introduced you to in Chapter Two. In article 1, it states that '[a] child means every human being below the age of 18 years unless under the law applicable to the child, majority is attained earlier'.

The UNCRC was adopted by the United Nations General Assembly in 1989 and was ratified by all countries except for Somalia and the United States (US). As we stated in Chapter Two, the UNCRC also has two optional protocols attached to it. These refer to the involvement of children in armed conflict and also the sale of children, child prostitution and child pornography (now more acceptably known as the sexual exploitation of children). On 19 December 2011, the UNCRC introduced a third optional protocol. This relates to a communications procedure that will allow individual children the opportunity to raise complaints if their individual rights under the convention and its optional protocols are not met.

The UK ratified (accepted) the convention on 16 December 1991. This means that it has agreed to look after the rights of children and to afford them the special protection that they need and also to be accountable for this. The UNCRC is a legal document that is internationally binding on states that ratified it. Countries that ratified the convention should do all they can to ensure that they follow the principles within their national policies and guidance. As seen in Chapter Two, the UNCRC has four core principles. We briefly include them here again as we know how important reading things more than once is in order to remember them:

- non-discrimination;
- devotion to the best interests of the child;
- the right to life, survival and development;
- respect for the views of the child (UN, 1989).

Countries that ratified the convention must report periodically to the United Nations Committee on the Rights of the Child.

What is the United Nations Committee on the Rights of the Child?

The United Nations Committee on the Rights of the Child is a committee of independent experts who monitor the implementation of the UNCRC. All countries that ratified the convention must hand in regular reports to the committee stating what they have done for children in their country relating to the convention. Now the third protocol has been introduced, individual complaints from children will also be able to be dealt with.

To find out more about the convention, see the additional sources at the end of this chapter.

Within the UK, the age identified in article 1 of the UNCRC is echoed in some national policies and guidance; setting the age limit of childhood at 18. However, there are some inconsistencies both within the UK and across other countries. For example, the age of consent for sex in the UK is 16 but in Spain it is 12. The age of criminal responsibility in England is 10 but in Scotland it is eight. This was criticised by the United Nations Committee on the Rights of the Child in 2002 and also the European Human Rights Commissioner in 2005. The age of criminal responsibility ranges between 12 and 14 in other European countries.

Differing ages of criminal responsibility

7 – Nigeria, South Africa, Switzerland

8 – Scotland, Sri Lanka

10 – Australia, England, New Zealand, Northern Ireland, Wales

12 – Canada, Greece, the Netherlands, Turkey

13 – France

14 – Bulgaria, China, Germany, Italy, Romania

15 – Czech Republic, Denmark, Finland, New York (US), Norway, South Carolina (US), Sweden

16 – Japan, Poland, Spain, Texas (US)

18 – Belgium, Luxembourg and most US states

Source: http://news.bbc.co.uk/1/hi/uk/8565619.stm

How can this happen? How can there be different views of when a child can be considered to be criminally responsible across the world? How can the ratified UNCRC state that a child is someone under the age of 18 but then across the world the age of criminal responsibility is different? This is only one example of the inconsistency or different approach taken to 'when is a child a child?'. More of these contradictions are shared with you in Chapter Nine.

Pause for thought and reflection

Does this variation in the age of criminal responsibility sound as if the biological approach to what it means to be a child is the only force at play when we consider childhood and what it means to be a child?

Legislation develops in line with the economic, social and political realities within particular countries. This variability in legislation and policy responses to the period of childhood is indicative that another approach to childhood is available. This 'other' approach of looking at childhood is called 'social construction'. This approach is adhered to by various social scientists and historians, for example Ariès (1962), Hine (1999) and Savage (2007), who suggest that childhood and youth is a social construct. This means that childhood is seen through the filter of the social, political and economic environment in which the child is growing up. Therefore, according to this viewpoint, childhood is created or made, not by the age of a person, but by meaning and interpretation that is predominantly constructed by the dominant cultural values in a society. These dominant forces are the people or situations that have the most power in a society or that make decisions that impact on all members of that society. Dominant cultural values can be influenced by the political and economic climate in a country, which we will explore from another perspective in Chapter Nine, when we introduce you to Thompson's (2006) personal, cultural and structural (PCS) model.

Pause for thought and reflection

What was it like being a child in your country?

What memories do you have of your childhood?

Were there certain expectations on you in terms of behaviour and what you did in your free time?

If you know someone who has grown up in a country different from yours, ask them about their childhood.

What was it like being a child in their country?

Were there certain expectations on them in terms of behaviour and what they did in their free time?

If you don't know someone who grew up in a different country from yours, try to ask someone from a different culture or racial background or someone who is much older or younger than yourself.

Is this person's response the same as yours?

Childhood is dependent on the type and nature of the society into which a child is born. From what you have found out during this reflection point, would your experiences support this?

These dominant cultural values link with the theory of **constructionism**, which explains that a child's reality is constructed or created by the broader environment and context around the child. To summarise, therefore, 'reality' is constructed by how we interpret certain situations and the meaning that we attach to these situations. This perspective that childhood is socially constructed is not a new phenomenon: numerous research studies have explored the differing childhoods of children through time and also in different places. Wagg (1992, pp 151-2) wrote about Ariès' (1962) book, *Centuries of childhood*: 'This book established that childhood was a social construction, relative to particular cultures and historical epochs. Few informed observers now doubt that "children" in any given society are what that society has helped to make them.'

Ariès (1962), a historian, argued that in the Middle Ages (the 5th to the 15th centuries), the very idea of childhood was non-existent. Ariès found in his research that during the Middle Ages children were introduced to adult society as soon as they were old enough not to be physically dependent on other people. This was at about the age of seven. Ariès studied paintings of this time period as well as historical records to conduct his research. He noted that in these paintings children were not depicted as different or separate from adults but rather as 'mini adults'. As can be seen in Figure 3.1, they wore the same clothes as adults and interacted with them in play and also work. During this period, children began work much younger than they do today and they were seen as having the same skills and responsibilities as adults.

Figure 3.1: Children in the Middle Ages

Pause for thought and reflection

Can you think of other ways whereby we can find out about different time periods and events from the past? How can we find out information if the people who were involved are not alive any more?

Postman (1994) also stated that during the Middle Ages, seven was the age for integration into adult society as this is the age by when children have full command of speech (and language). The theology of the Catholic Church believes that seven is the age of reason and children should be able to distinguish between right and wrong at this age. This supports our earlier discussion concerning the age of criminal responsibility.

Shorter (1975), in his book *The making of the modern family*, stated that during the Middle Ages the mortality rates of children were very high. For this reason, parents and society were quite indifferent to children and neglect was prevalent. When people referred to their children they were often called 'it' (Shorter, 1975). Stone (1977, pp 651-2) confirmed this by stating: 'The omnipresence of death coloured affective relations at all levels of society, by reducing the amount of emotional capital available for prudent investment in any single individual, especially in such ephemeral creatures as infants'.

> People could not allow themselves to become too attached to something that was regarded as a probable loss. This is the reason for certain remarks which shock our present-day sensibility, such as Montaigne's observation: 'I have lost two or three children in their infancy, not without regret, but without great sorrow'. (Ariès, 1962, p 38)

This idea of a lack of emotional investment by parents was later challenged by Pollock (1983) and Houlbrooke (1984). They said that affection in the 16th and 17th centuries was evident. This minimal evidence of emotional commitment could also be a result of the fact that children weren't seen as a separate category but rather as 'mini adults'.

Pause for thought and reflection

Think about the reality in some of the world's poorest countries where **infant** mortality is still extremely high. Do you think that parents there invest the same amount of emotional energy into their children during infancy when the probability of them dying is so high?

De Mause (1974, p 2), in a survey concerning development of childhood, stated: 'The history of childhood is a nightmare from which we have only just begun to awaken. The further back in history one goes, the lower the level of child care, and the more likely children are to be killed, abandoned, beaten, terrorized and sexually abused.' This quote is linked to the social construction of childhood through history. This social construction of childhood changes in line with the economic climate, access to medicine and other factors within a country.

> There is little sorrow for the death of an infant up until the age of eight or nine months. Really, it is only after the baby is a year old that we begin to grieve ... the infant is without history. The infant's story is not yet made up; it has no shape to it. And so the loss is not a big one; it is not heavy. The death passes over one lightly, and it is soon and easily forgotten.... For that is how we come to love our babies, when they begin to show us who they are and what kind of being we now have here, we begin to see what kind of child he will be, wild or gentle, fast or slow, smart or cunning. As his history begins to gather around him, that's when, oh my God, we don't want him to leave us. (Scheper Hughes, 1992, p 438)

Postman (1994) suggested that the printing press changed the age of integration into adult society. Speech was not the requisite for taking part in life any more: reading became this requirement. Postman argued that childhood emerged with mass literacy, which was enabled by the invention of the printing press. Through this, societies were created in which some could read (are literate) and these are adults and some could not read (illiterate) and these are children. (This theory does not include the notion of illiterate adults though and unfortunately we do not have space to unpack this further in this book.) Therefore a new period was created during which time children had to learn to read: childhood. This prolonged dependency on others in order to gain the new skill of reading was necessary to engage in the wider world outside the protective immediate family and **childcare** environment.

Pause for thought and reflection

Do you think that this is still the case today? In your country, at what age do children learn to read? Are there other means for children to access information and the 'grown-up'/adult world outside their homes, schools or childcare? Using Postman's (1994) rationale, do you think that this will impact on childhood?

The agricultural era

During the pre-industrial period, boys worked on the farmland with their father and girls worked in and around the house alongside their mother. We know this from the evidence of coroners' reports. A coroner's report is created after a death and states the cause of death. Coroners' reports of the time period suggested that a large number of children's deaths were due to agricultural accidents that took place while at work (Coster, 2007).

Industrial Revolution (1750–1800)

During the **Industrial Revolution** the principal forms of employment moved from farm labour to industrialised labour, which mainly took place in factories and mines. This was necessitated as Britain and other countries moved to a market economy. Poorer families especially, needed the money that children could earn through working from as young as the age of four years old. Children in **working-class** families therefore had a very different childhood from that experienced by children with better-off parents. As seen in Figure 3.2, working-class children constituted very useful employment for very little wages!

Children also worked in a variety of other roles. In the UK, for example, boys often worked as chimney sweeps. These boys either came from the work houses or were bought by a master sweeper from their parents and trained in a type of apprenticeship. Children also worked by cleaning shoes, selling flowers and matches, as domestic servants, prostitutes and in whatever other roles were deemed necessary.

Figure 3.2: Victorian working-class children

Victorian childhood

Nobody's child, a poem by P.H. Case, 1867

Alone, in the dreary
pitiless street,
With my torn old dress
and bare cold feet,
All day I wandered
to and fro,
Hungry and shivering
and nowhere to go.

(cited in Corbett, 1981)

During the 19th century in Britain, a variety of different rules and Acts (legislation) were introduced to regulate children's working. These Acts improved working conditions and gradually reduced the hours that children could work. They also regulated the age at which children could start working. However, the idea of children working was still upheld to the public as an economic necessity – to provide vital income to families – but it was also framed as a means to keep children busy and out of trouble. The suggestion of constructionism during this stage lies in observations about how a minority (the ruling elite) was able to use and exploit the masses (majority). In general, what 'childhood' is, is therefore created by the cultural values of the dominant parties in a society. This links with the ideas of **Marxism** and **critical theory**.

Some of the historical legislation governing children's lives in the UK

- *1802:* the Health and Morals of Apprentices Act – limited the work of children in textile mills – 12 hours a day; no night work; set minimum standards for living accommodation; some elementary education had to be provided.
- *1833:* the Mills and Factories Act (Althorp's Act) – younger children had to attend school at least two hours a day, six days a week; holidays were given sparingly and consisted of all day on Christmas Day and Good Friday and eight other half-days.
- *1874:* the Factory Act – raised the minimum working age to nine; women and children were only allowed to work for 10 hours a day in the textile industry and this work had to take place between the hours of 6am and 6pm; the working week was also reduced to 56.5 hours.

The equivalents of the Factory Acts in the UK were the Child Labour Laws in the US. Child labour around the rest of the world has also been impacted on by conventions and laws. In 1973, a number of countries ratified the Minimum Age Convention as set out by the **International Labour Organization**. The suggested age range for children entering employment in this convention ranges from 14 to 16. Article 32 of the UNCRC also speaks out against child labour.

Article 32 of the UNCRC

'1. States Parties recognize the right of the child to be protected from economic exploitation and from performing any work that is likely to be hazardous or to interfere with the child's education, or to be harmful to the child's health or physical, mental, spiritual, moral or social development.

2. States Parties shall take legislative, administrative, social and educational measures to ensure the implementation of the present article. To this end, and having regard to the relevant provisions of other international instruments, States Parties shall in particular:

(a) Provide for a minimum age or minimum ages for admission to employment;
(b) Provide for appropriate regulation of the hours and conditions of employment;
(c) Provide for appropriate penalties or other sanctions to ensure the effective enforcement of the present article.'

Modern childhood

In modern society, childhood is seen as distinct and different from adulthood and it is expected that children are 'protected from or kept separate' from the adult world. Several reasons can be found for the creation of a modern childhood. These are:

- industrialisation and the subsequent invention of the printing press – the world now needs an educated workforce;
- laws restricting child labour, for example the Minimum Age Convention of 1973;

■ the introduction of compulsory education but also the raising of the participation age. For example, in Australia the schooling and education of children are governed by the local governments of each individual state. There is therefore a difference in school-leaving ages across the Australian states, ranging from 15 to 17 years of age. In Europe, this differentiation in school-leaving ages ranges from 16 in the UK and Spain to 18 in Belgium, Italy, the Netherlands and Poland. It is therefore clear that there is a disparity in the participation ages across the world;

■ laws that apply specifically to children, for example laws to do with age of criminal responsibility, age of consent and so on;

■ the development of an economic market directly focused on children, for example television, toys, food, books, clothes, social network sites and games for children. Postman (1994) thought that television and computers were modern tools that enabled children to access the adult world. Reading was therefore no longer the only way for children to access this world. These media sources also increased the marketing **demographic** to include and target children as a 'marketing demographic' in their own right;

■ Child Protection Acts, for example, the Children and Young Persons Act 1933, the Children Act 1989 and the Children Act 2004 in England and Wales. Globally, the UNCRC was the starting point for more focused local laws and policies (NSPCC, 2012).

All these aspects create and reinforce a separate childhood distinct and different from adulthood, with different rights, responsibilities and expectations. As suggested earlier in this chapter, this social construction does not only happen through time but also in different geographical areas. However, this modern idea of socially constructed, extended childhood is not found in all **cultures** and societies around the world.

Wagg (1992) argues that although children worldwide go through the same stages of biological and physical development, different cultures will define differently or give different meaning to these stages. Therefore, even today, some societies or cultures might not see a difference between childhood and adulthood. In some societies the notion of childhood is more similar to what Ariès (1962) observed in the Middle Ages. To help refresh your mind, he commented that as soon as a child is largely independent and has the ability to communicate fluently then they are considered to be able to take on adult roles.

Pause for thought and reflection

Can you think of any examples of this (either in your own society or the rest of the world)?

Don't worry if you can't as this chapter will go further to identify some diverse examples of the realities of some children's childhood.

A number of films have been produced in which this social and cultural construction of childhood in today's wider world is evident. At the time of writing, the most recent and thought provoking of these is *Africa united*. This is a story about three children who are making their way from Rwanda to Johannesburg, South Africa to enable one of the trio to partake in the Football World Cup opening ceremony in 2010. Along the way it becomes evident that the brother and sister pair are **HIV/AIDS** orphans living in a squatter camp reliant only on themselves and each other. Their friend is a direct contrast as his parents are rich and he lives in a big house and attends school. Along their journey to South Africa they befriend a child soldier in the Congo and an adolescent female sex worker in Malawi. Unbeknownst to the rest of the children the boy looking after his sister is HIV positive and he is taking constant medication to keep himself healthy. His sister wants to become a doctor but does not have access to schooling as they both have to beg for money to stay alive. Even though this is a fictional film, the cultural construction of the roles highlights the realities of childhood within some contemporary cultural and economic contexts.

What follows are a few examples of these constructed childhoods in countries across the world. They are by no means exhaustive, and we challenge you to actively seek and make others aware of these alternative constructions of childhood throughout the world.

According to the UN Secretary General's Special Representative on Children and Armed Conflict, child soldiers are a reality not only in some African countries, for example the Congo and Northern Sudan but also in other countries, for example Nepal. In some cases these children are abducted and forced to fight but in the majority of cases they join for a variety of reasons, for example for material gain, they believe in the group's **ideology**, for revenge as perhaps a family member was killed, or because they just want to leave their family home. Even though there are a number of reasons why children become soldiers, this can only happen if the leadership of the army or group allows this to happen. Therefore, it is clear that the social or cultural construction of the society or group in which this happens plays a major role in whether a child can become a child soldier or not (Coomaraswamy, 2009).

> When we got there we were in an ambush, the rebels were attacking where we were in the bush. I did not shoot my gun at first, but when you looked around and saw your schoolmates, some younger than you, crying while they were dying with their blood spilling all over you, there was no option but to start pulling the trigger. The sight stays with you. I was just pulling the trigger. I lost my parents during the war, they told us to join the army to avenge our parents. (Kruger, 2001)

The reality of childhood for millions of children in Sub-Saharan Africa cannot be more different than that of children in developed countries. HIV/AIDS claims millions of lives in Sub-Saharan Africa, leaving behind vulnerable children who have not only physical needs, for example nutrition and healthcare, but also emotional needs: 'My sister is six years old. There are no grown-ups living with us. I need a bathroom tap and clothes and shoes. And water also, inside the house. But especially, somebody to tuck me and my sister in at night-time' (Apiwe, aged 13, cited in IRIN News, 2003).

It is clear that childhood and how it is constructed changes throughout time but is also different in different countries. As practitioners it is important for us to remember this and to be aware of the cultural backgrounds of the children, young people and families who we work with. We must not make assumptions about the lived realities of any of the people we work with but listen and respond sensitively to their own unique experiences and backgrounds. In Chapter Five we introduce you to the skills needed to work effectively with children and young people, which includes listening. In Chapter Nine we address further how to work with difference and **diversity**.

Social construction of youth

A lot of what we have already discussed in this chapter is relevant for young people as well as children. Youth as a social and cultural construction became more evident through the work of G. Stanley Hall. He was the first to study adolescence as a life stage separate from childhood.

Young people are often fully grown and physically mature at some stage during their secondary school years. However, (western) society still sees them as 'immature' and labels them as 'teenagers', 'young people', 'adolescents' or 'youths'. They are still included in the definition for a child as defined by the UNCRC. The term 'adolescence' was first used in 1904 by G. Stanley Hall (Hall, 1904). Hall made a distinction between the social construct of **adolescence** and the biological period of **puberty**. Puberty is a universal reality for all people across the world as every person's body changes to allow for sexual maturity and reproduction. However, as we have seen with childhood, adolescence or youth is not universal but a socially constructed reality.

During the early 20th century, it was perceived that reform was needed in American society. Problems of youth deviance were evident and people who wanted things to change asked the government to intervene. These interventions came in the form of making education mandatory for longer. Hall supported these reforms as he felt that delaying young people's entry into the world of work would be beneficial and an extended education would develop and refine the 'savage' young people (Savage, 2007, pp 66-7). Hall's 'adolescence' allowed for societal norms and expectations of young people to change. Instead of expecting adolescents to be out working and contributing to the economy by a certain age, young people or adolescents were now granted an 'extended childhood' period.

Prolonged compulsory education became a means to keep young people 'children' for longer. Compulsory education mostly takes place within school settings (except where, for example, children are home-schooled) and this leads to segregation between different age groups of children but also keeps children largely separate from adults and the adult world. Therefore, learning and social interaction take place within a carefully constructed age and peer group (Chudacoff, 1989). This is further reinforced by school-run activities and after-school sport and leisure.

Pause for thought and reflection

Think back to your own adolescent years. Think about who you considered to be your peers and who you considered to be your friends. What made some people your peers and what made others your friends?

Your peers are the people who are the same age as you and therefore in your class or form at school. Your friends could be part of your peer group but are the people who you have more in common with, such as a shared love for a sport, activity, type of music and so on.

Let's reflect back on the idea that the social construction of childhood and youth is a result of the economic, cultural and social reality of a country. In England the participation age (with regard to participation in education or training) has recently been raised from 16. From 2013, young people must stay in education or training until the end of the academic year in which they turn 17. From 2015, young people will have to stay in education or training until the end of the academic year in which they turn 18. This does not mean that they have to stay in school but that they have to access some form of education or training, through for example an apprenticeship, part-time education or training, school, college or home-schooling (DfE, 2012a). This is a direct result of the economic situation in the UK and the extent of unemployment, especially for young people.

During the 1950s and 1960s, the term 'teenager' became popular. Teenagers became a unique and, as we stated earlier, marketable demographic in their own right. According to Hine (1999), consumerism was a double-edged sword. It relied on this separateness between adults and young people; however, it also reified (made real) divisions between adults and young people.

Concerns with regard to drugs, sex, politics and religion drove the generations apart. The media publicised what young people were up to and this led to these concerns spreading widely. Power over and control of young people up to the age of 18 became more the norm and reality.

It is therefore clear that the period of adolescence and youth is also socially constructed. Not just throughout time but also in different countries. To reiterate what we shared with you earlier in this chapter, it is important for practitioners working with children and young people to have a working knowledge of the social construction of childhood and youth. Due to globalisation and the movement of people across the world, we, as practitioners, need to be aware that not all children, young people or their parents have had the same experiences as us. As we will explore further in Chapter Nine, not all children and young people are from the same social and cultural background and therefore will bring with them a huge variety of life experiences – both positive and challenging. By being aware of the varied realities of childhood and youth, we can start working in collaboration with children and young people from where they are at, not only physically but also emotionally. We will explore this point more specifically in Chapter Eight.

SUMMARY OF KEY POINTS

In this chapter we have started to explore:

- the two different ways to consider childhood and youth;
- the biological or physical reality of childhood and puberty as universal;
- the social and cultural construction of childhood and youth;
- the notion that the social construction of childhood has developed throughout history and is still developing.
- the notion that the social construction of childhood and youth is situated not only in time but also in place, meaning that children in different countries and cultures also have different realities of childhood.

FURTHER READING

A good, clear introduction to the concept of social construction: Berger, P.L. and Luckmann, T. (1966) *The social construction of reality*, Garden City, NY: Anchor Books.

A book that provides an introduction to the concepts and theories relating to working with young children and childhood, and fully unpacks the theory around the social construction of childhood as well as the impact of this on practice: Maynard, T. and Thomas, N. (2009) *An introduction to early childhood studies* (2nd edn), London: Sage Publications.

A book that makes the links between education and the construction of childhood – a useful text if you are interested in formal or informal education: Blundell, D. (2011) *Education and constructions of childhood*, London: Continuum International Publishing Group Ltd.

ONLINE RESOURCES

For a plain English explanation of all the UNCRC articles, go to:

www.un.org/cyberschoolbus/humanrights/index.asp

To read more about HIV/AIDS and how it impacts on people and especially children around the world, we suggest you look at the website of AVERTing HIV and AIDS, an international HIV/AIDS charity (www.avert.org).

To find out more about UNICEF and its work, we suggest that you browse its website (www.unicef.org).

4

child and adolescent development

Introduction

This chapter will outline some of the key theories and concepts regarding child and adolescent development. You might wonder why it is necessary to explore child development theory in a book with the main focus on working with children and young people. We feel strongly that it is necessary to not only have good practical skills in working with children and young people but also to have a sound theoretical basis that underpins the skills used in our field of work. For example, knowing what developmental stage or phase a child is in will allow us to interact with and explore the child's world with them in a developmentally appropriate manner. It is important to not only focus on theories but also to look at the individual child's circumstances and reality. All children are unique and we must use our observation and communication skills to successfully work with each individual child or young person. We introduce these and other skills in Chapter Five.

Defining development

What do we mean when we say we are going to explore child and adolescent development? Child and adolescent development refers to the physical and also psychological changes that a child goes through from conception right through to the end of adolescence.

As there are many different theories relating to child and adolescent development, we will focus on the theories that will provide you with a sound theoretical starting point in exploring some of the different areas of development. The main areas to be explored with the theorists to be included are presented in Table 4.1

Table 4.1: Theories of child development

Main development area	Main theorist
Cognitive development (intellectual development)	Piaget
Socio-cognitivism	Vygotsky
Behaviourism – Classical conditioning – Operant conditioning	Pavlov Skinner
Social learning theory	Bandura
Psychosocial development	Erikson
Social and emotional development	Bowlby

As there is enough information on each of these to fill a number of books, we will briefly explore each area and signpost you to further reading at the end of the chapter that will be beneficial in further expanding your knowledge and understanding. A key insight to have with regard to the theory that informs your practice is that all theories have criticism and it is important not just to accept a theory at face value. As you progress in your studies, the phrase 'critical analysis' will be introduced to you. This means to critically evaluate and unpack a theory to identify its strengths and weaknesses but also to identify a theory that will address the weaknesses. Theories can work together to explain development and behaviour. We work with people, all with individual and unique life experiences and therefore we must always engage with the whole individual and not just focus on one aspect or theory in isolation.

Cognitive development

Cognitive development refers to the development of the intellectual capabilities of a person. The first person to study cognitive development was Jean Piaget, a Swiss psychologist, during the 1920s. He was also trained in biology and philosophy and this impacted on his approach.

Piaget's (2001) theory is a constructivist theory. This means that the child actively constructs (or makes) knowledge out of the experiences that they have. You came across this term in Chapter Three when we looked at the social construction of childhood. This theory suggest that the child is not a passive learner, in other words they don't just learn because things happen to them, but rather they are discovering how the world works through simple tests – 'child as scientist' (Maynard and Thomas, 2009, p 65). In other words, a child may repeat the same action more than once to see if the result is consistently the same. It is like a scientist in a laboratory doing an experiment more than once to see if the result stays the same.

According to Piaget's theory there are four stages of cognitive development. They follow on from each other and the later stages of development build on the success of the earlier stages. According to Piaget, all children go through these stages in the same order, irrespective of how quickly or slowly they progress through the stages. Piaget's theory hold that parents, teachers and others are there to set up learning experiences for children but only when a child is ready to learn will the information and knowledge be learnt.

The first stage in Piaget's theory of cognitive development is the **sensorimotor** stage. According to the theory, this lasts from birth up to about two years of age. During this stage, children are mostly reflexive (impulsive like a knee-jerk response – without really thinking about it) and responses are automatic. Children learn through these responses and physical actions. Through **assimilation**, **accommodation** and **equilibrium**, infants build increasingly more complex and detailed sensorimotor **schemas**. Schemas are 'patterns of repeatable actions that lead to early categories and then logical classifications' (Athey, 1990, p 36), for example new experiences are assimilated (included) through integration (combining) with what the baby knows already. Therefore assimilation takes place if the situation fits in with something already known. Accommodation happens when an infant (or anyone else for that matter) has to change or adapt their response to a new experience because it doesn't fit in with their schema – what they already know about the world and how it works. Finally, equilibrium is when the infant aims to find the balance between assimilation and accommodation to create what can be seen as a stable understanding (Maynard and Thomas, 2009).

During this stage, infants start to differentiate themselves from objects. They see that they are separate from objects and other people. They realise that they are an **agent** of action themselves and they start to act intentionally, for example shaking a rattle to make a noise or pressing a button on a toy to get a response. This agency allows for babies to be the instigators of cause and effect. Cause and effect means that certain actions lead to certain outcomes

During this stage infants also achieve **object permanence**. This is the realisation that things continue to exist even when the baby can't see, hear or touch them any more. For example, infants start to realise that if their mother or another main carer leaves the room it does not mean that she does not exist any more. Before infants achieve object permanence they think that if they can't see an object or a person then it does not exist any more. This makes for hours of fun playing peek a boo with an infant, but is not much fun when a parent wants to go to the toilet!

Pause for thought and reflection

Separation anxiety is where the infant gets upset and cries when their main carer leaves the room. Do you think there is a link between an infant who has not yet reached object permanence and what is called 'separation anxiety'?

By the age of two, most children have entered the **pre-operational phase**. This phase continues roughly to the age of seven. During this stage, children learn to use language and also that they can represent objects by using images and words. During this stage, children's thinking can be described as reflective rather than just merely **reflexive**. They can mentally represent an object that is not there at the time, for example drawings of people, houses, cars and so on. Piaget calls this **symbolic function**. It can also be observed in children's copying of others and also their make-believe play, for example, children taking an old cardboard box and transforming it into a train simply by getting into it and making the appropriate train gestures and sounds, or children dressing up in their mother's or father's clothes and playing they are adults, taking on their perceived roles and behaviours. During this stage, children will firmly believe in the tooth fairy, the Easter bunny and also Father Christmas.

Figure 4.1: Dressed-up child

The pre-operational phase is one of the most creative and lovely phases to watch. Another very interesting focus area of this stage is called **animism**. This is the tendency to give life-like qualities to non-living things, for example giving names, personalities and feelings to dolls and soft toys. Another example of this is when a child, for example, bumps their toe against a stair and then says that the stair is naughty. Thinking is still very egocentric, meaning that during this stage, children have difficulty accepting the viewpoints and perspectives of other people.

Pause for thought and reflection

How do you think this difficulty to accept the viewpoints and perspectives of others impacts on play with other children? How can you, as a practitioner, appropriately respond to egocentrism during this phase? It is important to realise that your response will be different from that with a child in a further stage of cognitive development.

Pre-operational children tend to classify objects together that they have defined by a single feature. For example, they will group together all the red vehicles regardless of what type of vehicles they are or they will group together all the construction vehicles (in Bob the Builder for example) regardless of their individual colour.

The next stage in Piaget's theory of cognitive development is the **concrete operational stage**. This typically takes place during the ages of seven to 11. During this stage, children can think logically about objects and events. They achieve **conservation** of number, mass and weight. This means that they realise that the quantity, number or length of an item is not related to how it is displayed. As an example of this we can refer to Piaget's conservation experiment (see Figure 4.2). In this experiment, Piaget placed two containers in front of a child that had not reached the concrete operational stage and asked what container contained the highest volume of water. Both containers were filled with the same volume. He then took one of the containers and in front of the child poured the liquid into a differently shaped container. He asked the child again which container contained the most liquid. The child stated that the container that was filled to the highest level contained

Figure 4.2: Piaget's conservation task

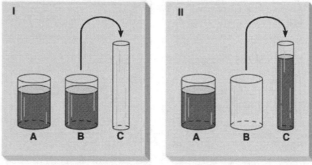

Source: Piaget (2001)

the most liquid. This was regardless of the fact that Piaget took one of the two equally filled containers and poured all the liquid from it into a differently shaped container in front of the child. Therefore, it should be clear that it contained exactly the same volume even though it now looked different as it was displayed in a differently shaped container. During the concrete operational stage, children are able to 'see' that both containers still contain the same volume of liquid regardless of the shape of the container.

During the concrete operational stage, children become able to classify objects according to more than one feature and they can also order objects in a series along a single dimension, for example size. They are interested in things that they can experience with their senses, for example what they can see and touch in the physical environment. During this stage, children are unable to think abstractly about situations and they are unable to systematically test out a **hypothesis**. To help you understand this more, please see the first example in the next stage.

According to Piaget, at around 12 years of age, children enter the **formal operational stage**. During this stage, children can think logically about abstract ideas and they are also able to formulate and test hypotheses in a scientific manner. A good example here is the pendulum experiment (see Figure 4.3). During this experiment,

Figure 4.3: Piaget's pendulum experiment

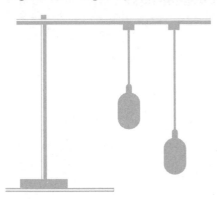

Source: Piaget (2001)

children have to determine what has the biggest impact on the speed of the swing of a pendulum. Three **variables** (things that can change) are involved in making the pendulum swing: first, the length of the string; second, the mass of the weights attached; and last, the force exerted to make the pendulum swing. Children who have reached the formal operational stage would test these variables one at a time. Therefore they would test it systematically. Children who are not in formal operations would change more than one variable at a time. For example, they would change the speed of the swing and the mass of the weights at the same time. Children who have reached the formal operational stage are able to think and act systematically, abstractly and logically. According to Piaget, they will see how changing any one aspect will have an impact and therefore they would 'test' only one change at a time. They are therefore able to see relationships between different aspects (Inhelder and Piaget, 1958).

During the formal operational stage, children are able to move from the concrete to the abstract in their thinking. Therefore, they are able to start thinking about thinking itself. This is known as 'meta-cognition'. They are also able to think about love, religion, for example faith, and other more abstract concepts (Arnett, 2010). Children who are not yet at this stage are unable to do this.

As mentioned at the start of this chapter, no academic theory is without its criticism and shortcomings. Piaget's theory is no exception. This is not necessarily a bad thing; it is simply part of the process of knowledge creation and development. A good way to explain it is to think that one person creates a theory; others then try it out and then include further or other aspects in order to make it better or to show that other aspects are more or equally important or relevant in different ways. Theories tend to follow on from each other and extend thinking. We will see this clearly when we identify some of the criticisms of Piaget's theory and then look at further theories relating to cognitive development. However, this does not mean that the original theory is not valuable any more.

A criticism of Piaget's theory is that he did not take into account memory or language limitations that can impact on individual children. According to Piaget, language does not have a role in the process of learning or structuring thinking. He also did not take into account the contribution of social interaction in the development of children's thinking. Even though his theory asserts that by roughly the age of 12, children reach the formal operations phase, this is not necessarily the case. Piaget did not acknowledge that not all people achieve the formal operational stage or that some people use formal operations in some thinking processes but not in others.

Regardless of the criticism, Piaget's theory of cognitive development is still widely used as a starting point. It provides us with a sound basis to think about cognitive development and your further studies on cognitive development will build on Piaget's theory. The next group of theories includes the social interaction that Piaget's theory was criticised for not including.

Socio-cognitivism or social constructivism

A further group of theorists believe that the development of the cognitive skills of reasoning and learning is not only the result of learning opportunities set by, for example, parents or school and being able and ready to learn the information presented. They believe that informal social interactions between people are also important for cognitive development. When people are socially interacting, language is necessary to communicate (communication skills will be addressed further in Chapter Five). This group of theories therefore incorporates two aspects that Piaget was criticised for: lack of importance attached to social interaction and also language limitations.

The Russian, Lev Vygotsky, believed that social interaction is needed for learning and that this includes verbal as well as written language (Vygotsky, 1962). Language creates cognitive, but also socially and culturally, constructed realities that impact on and shape how people see the world. This links with what we explored in Chapter Two concerning the social construction of childhood. Language is a vehicle that facilitates the transmission and spread of socially constructed ideas and patterns of behaviour.

Words are part of the thought process and these change and develop throughout life. As children grow and have more and broader experiences, they also gain a bigger vocabulary. Children's experiences and vocabulary therefore expand as they attend, for example, music groups or messy playgroups, start preschool or attend another setting outside their homes. Children then move on to school and other further activities that expose them to a wider vocabulary and more varied experiences. But until such times, how can a child describe a feeling if they do not know the word or words for that feeling? This is something that we, as practitioners, must give consideration to in our practice. Children are not always aware of the names of the full range of emotions and therefore can struggle to verbalise what they are feeling. Beyond feeling happy, cross or bored, there are further, more complex emotions, including frustration, jealousy, excitement and nervousness. This is where a teaching resource, for example an emotion board or emotion sticker, to put next to their name when they come to your session or project is useful. You can use this as an opportunity to discuss with them what is important to them at the start of the day or something that might have upset them or made them happy, for example the death of a beloved pet, the birth of a new member of the family, a parent travelling for work and so on. This can then inform you as to how to interact with them through the day, as appropriate. This will expose children to the language and meaning of a broader range of emotions and also make your practice more effective.

Pause for thought and reflection

How can preschool and primary school teachers develop children's knowledge and understanding of their own as well as others' emotions? Bear in mind that during the pre-operational stage, children are egocentric.

According to Vygotsky, there is a difference in the level of learning that children can achieve alone and the learning that they can achieve when someone more knowledgeable helps or supports them. This is called the **zone of proximal development**. The development of shared language (language that is understood by the practitioner

Figure 4.4: Graphical representation of the zone of the proximal 'development'

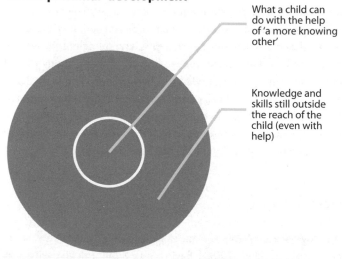

What a child can do with the help of 'a more knowing other'

Knowledge and skills still outside the reach of the child (even with help)

and the child) is necessary for practitioners to encourage children to enter a zone of proximal development. Therefore, in contrast to what Piaget said, practitioners and others who are more knowledgeable (for example parents) can make a difference to the rate at which children learn new things.

Pause for thought and reflection

What is the implication of what Vygotsky is saying about shared language for people working with children and young people?

What does this imply for the way that we speak to the children and young people who we work with across the whole age range of childhood?

Behaviourism

Another group of theorists suggest that children learn through making connections between different events or making connections between a cause and an effect – also known as an action and its consequence. Behaviourism is not a developmental theory but it provides us with insight into how new behaviour is acquired or learned. It is therefore a learning theory. Behaviourism is a **positivist,** scientific way of looking at the world and these theorists avoid feelings, thoughts and emotions and rather focus on what can be observed and statistically represented and recreated in a controlled experimental environment (Beckett and Taylor, 2010). In other words, if you were to repeat the same experiment more than once in exactly the same manner under the same conditions, you should get the same results.

Classical conditioning

Pavlov's dogs are probably the most famous dogs connected to an academic study (Raiker, 2007)! Pavlov was a physiologist who was interested in the digestive system. He found that dogs started to salivate at the sight or smell of food and that this was a reflex action that took place without the dog being able to control it. This reflexion action can be seen in humans, for example in the way children (or adults) automatically put their hands out when they fall over to break their fall or involuntarily pull their hands back if they touch a hot stove.

Pavlov rang a buzzer every time the dogs in the experiment were fed. Eventually the dogs started to salivate just by hearing the buzzer, even if there was no food forthcoming! The involuntary salivating reflex had been conditioned or trained to take place in response to a new stimulus – the buzzer – rather than the original stimulus – the food. This is a conditioned reflex and Pavlov named it 'classical conditioning' (Beckett and Taylor, 2010). According to Pavlov and other behaviourists, for example Thorndike (1905, in Nevid, 2012), learning is mechanical and thinking is not part of the process.

Operant conditioning

Burrhus Frederic, or 'B.F.', Skinner's operant conditioning works from the principle that if you reward specific behaviour it will be repeated and if you punish certain behaviour it will decrease (Skinner, 1938).

Pause for thought and reflection

To what extent have you seen or experienced this before – as a child, as a parent or as a practitioner working with children or young people?

Think about:

■ super nanny and the use of naughty steps for unacceptable behaviour and reward sticker charts for positive behaviour within the home environment;

- the use of stickers or golden time in primary schools to encourage positive behaviour.

Operant conditioning involves positive reinforcement and negative reinforcement. Good behaviour is rewarded and negative or wrong behaviour is 'punished' or negatively reinforced.

Pause for thought and reflection

It is important for parents and practitioners to emphasise that it is the behaviour that is unacceptable or naughty rather than the child who is naughty. Why do you think this is necessary?

Observation and social learning theory

Observation forms part of how children learn. Children observe behaviour and then learn from it.

Albert Bandura's (1977) Bobo doll experiment explored how children learn through observation. During the experiment one of three groups of children observed an adult hitting a Bobo doll with a mallet. When the children in this group had an opportunity (without the adult in the room) to go close to the Bobo doll, the majority of them also hit the doll with the mallet. This experiment is used to show (or evidence) that children learn through observing the behaviour of others. According to this theory, children will copy behaviour that they see. Behaviour that children observe can be either positive or negative and can be displayed by either a same-sex or different-sex role model. In general, children tend to copy same-sex role models more than different-sex role models (Bandura, 1977). This example also makes clear that role models can not only be positive but can also be negative. This is an often neglected point in discussions of practitioner role models.

Pause for thought and reflection

Do you think that aggressive behaviour in children can be explained by aggressive behaviour in a parent at home?

What position would this place a practitioner in who works with a particular child?

Alternatively, think about the shortage of male role models; either in single-parent families or in early years education and primary schools.

What impact do you think this might have on a child, especially boys?

As practitioners we have to ensure that we always display positive and appropriate behaviour. Why? Because children, young people, their families or the rest of the community may be observing us. We have to ensure that we are positive role models.

Pause for thought and reflection

Do you think that it can be expected that you must *always* act as a role model? With 'always' we mean every day, even if you are on holiday. If yes, why? If not, why not?

Psychosocial development

Erik Erikson (1968) also identified stages of human development but focused on other aspects such as identity and personality development. His research led to recognition of an eight-stage theory about human **psychosocial** development. (For the purposes of this book we will focus on the first six stages as the last two stages concern middle and late adulthood and fall outside our remit.) Psychosocial refers to the **psychological** and social aspects that impact on personality and behaviour from birth. It is important to note that Erikson's theory is only one of a number of relevant theories and as with other theories (note Piaget above) it is not without criticism and limitations. However, it provides a sound starting point to discuss **identity** as part of psychosocial development. Each of the eight stages he identified represents a distinct age range. According to Erikson, each stage has a separate issue or 'crisis' that needs to be resolved. Erikson believed that every stage must be completed successfully for the positive **ego development outcome** to be reached, before moving on to the next stage.

Erikson's first stage of psychosocial development is the oral sensory stage or infancy. According the theory, this ranges from birth to 18 months. This stage is so named because babies tend to put things in their mouths. The mouth is very sensitive in babies and because babies do not have **fine motor control** over their hands and individual fingers they pick things up and put it in their mouths with their fists. From there they can explore the object with their lips, tongue and gums. This can continue well into a child's second year. During this stage the most constant caregiver (usually but not always the mother) will be the most significant person that the child has a relationship with. The issue or crisis that needs to be resolved during this stage is that of trust versus mistrust. According to Erikson, if a child feels that their physical and emotional needs are being met during this stage, they will be able to trust people and form trusting relationships in later life. If constant frustration, due to needs not being met, is the norm during this stage, then the child will not develop the ability to trust and according to Erikson they might end up feeling worthless and mistrust other people.

Pause for thought and reflection

Controlled crying is a method used to teach babies how to fall asleep without being fed, held or cuddled. In the method, if the baby cries, the parent will go in to the room, comfort them without picking them up and then leave the room. The length of time the parent will leave before going back in (if the baby continues to cry) becomes slightly longer and longer until hopefully the baby falls asleep. Using Erikson's theory of psychosocial development, how do you think this practice might impact on the ego development outcome during the oral sensory stage?

Erikson's second stage of psychosocial development is named **early childhood** and, according to the theory, incorporates 18 months up until three years of age. The crisis or issue that needs to be overcome is that of autonomy versus shame. During this stage, children learn to walk, talk and also feed themselves. Fine motor development also takes place and children gain control over their bodies and acquire a great number of skills. According to Erikson, children have the opportunity to build their self-esteem and also autonomy. Just think about the phrase 'terrible twos'. At this age, children are learning to assert themselves and this can be observed through the constant use of the word 'no', which shows development of the will. In developing this autonomy, they need to overcome the issue of shame, embarrassment and doubting themselves and their abilities. If they become embarrassed or humiliated during the process of learning important skills, for example using the toilet or feeding themselves, they may doubt their own capabilities and low self-esteem could be the result of this.

Pause for thought and reflection

What do you think is the impact of trying to potty-train a child before they are 'ready'?

As a practitioner working with this age range, what would you suggest to parents who started to potty-train their child a week ago and the child is unable to stay dry or clean at all?

Erikson's third stage is called **early school** and this covers ages three to five years. The crisis or issue that needs to be overcome during this stage is that of initiative versus guilt. During this stage, children copy adults through role play and they take the initiative in creating different play situations. Children experiment with what they believe it means to be an adult. Think back to the 'Pause for thought and reflection' concerning the lack of male role models in early and primary education. A question that is frequently asked during this stage is 'why?', which is used to explore and make sense of the world.

A poem about why children ask 'why?'

Why do children ask why?
Why is there night and day?
Why are the rain clouds grey?
Why did the dinosaurs come and go?
Why is it slippery when there's snow?
Don't they know?
They'll soon learn, they just have to wait until it's their turn.

(Reece Wells, age 10)

During this stage, children become involved in social role identification. This includes **gender** role identification. If during this stage they are frustrated over natural desires and goals, they may experience guilt – guilt that they are not feeling or experiencing what is deemed to be natural or normal for their age. During this stage, the most significant relationships are with the basic family.

Pause for thought and reflection

How do you think children learn about their gender and what is perceived as acceptable behaviour or not for their gender?

Sandra Lipsitz Bem is a psychologist who developed the well-known gender schema theory and shows how people use this to organise aspects of their life. This theory is used to identify male, female or androgynous characteristics in people. If you are interested in this, the full article is listed in the References (Bem, 1981). Bem's gender schema theory is developed from a combination of cognitive development theory and social learning theory.

School age or **middle childhood** is the fourth stage in Erikson's theory of psychosocial development. This is also called **latency** and incorporates the ages of six to 12 years. During this stage, the issue or crisis that needs to be resolved is that of industry versus inferiority. During middle childhood, children experience a lot of new responsibilities in terms of learning and also gradually become more responsible. They are becoming more aware of their individuality and their confidence grows as their sphere of influence increases and stretches beyond the family. According to Erikson, if this stage is not successfully completed children may feel that they are not good enough or inadequate. It is important to remember that there are other theories available on this topic area that you will come across in future studies.

The fifth stage in Erikson's theory is adolescence, which according to the theory covers ages 12 to 18. The crisis in this stage is that of identity versus role confusion. During this stage of adolescent psychosocial development, young people are developing their own identity. The simplest way to define identity is 'who I am in relation to someone else'. If a young person is unable to develop their own identity during adolescence then role confusion will be the end result. In other words, when the young person reaches adulthood they will not have a clear sense of who they are and their place in the world. During adolescence the actions of young people (the things that they choose to do themselves) become more important than what they have always been told to do. According to Erikson's theory, as young people increasingly assert their independence, their most significant relationships are with their friends. This interaction with friends is increasingly important in order for them to decide what is important and who they want to be, rather than who they have been told they are in previous years. This interaction with friends is therefore a crucial part of identity formation.

Pause for thought and reflection

Thinking about Erikson's theory and the increased importance of friends in the lives of adolescents, who do you think are best placed to provide advice and support to a young person? A practitioner or another young person who has relevant life experiences who can act as a peer mentor or engage in peer education?

The stage after adolescence, the sixth stage, is known as young adulthood. This stage ranges from the age of 18 up to 35. After the identity formation stage of adolescence, young people are able to consider companionship and intimacy in the next stage of their psychosocial development. According to Erikson's theory, if this stage is successful, young people will be able to experience both intimacy and significant relationships with life partners and friends that are rewarding. From Erikson's perspective, if this stage is not successful young adults may well experience isolation. Thus, the crisis in this stage is that between intimacy and solidarity and isolation.

Table 4.2 contains a summary of Erikson's eight stages of psychosocial development.

Table 4.2: Summary of Erikson's stages of psychosocial development

Age	Stage	Ego development outcome
Birth-8 months	Infancy	Trust versus mistrust
18 months-3 years	Early childhood	Autonomy versus shame
3-5 years	Early school	Initiative versus guilt
6-12 years	Middle childhood	Industry versus inferiority
12-18 years	Adolescence	Identity versus role confusion
18-35 years	Young adulthood	Intimacy and solidarity versus isolation
35-55/65 years	Middle adulthood	Generativity versus self-absorption stagnation
55/65 to death	Late adulthood	Integrity versus despair

Attachment theory

Another extremely important and influential theory is John Bowlby's (1969) **attachment theory**. This is still influential today and upheld as an important theory in relation to child development and the formation of social relationships. But what is attachment theory?

Attachment refers to an emotional bond with another person. Bowlby's attachment theory relates to the special emotional bond and relationship that a young child shares with their primary carer. Bowlby believed that experiences that children have in early childhood will have an influence on later development. According to Bowlby, a child's first attachment is normally with their mother. If the mother cares for the child and provides for both physical and emotional needs, thereby creating a safe and caring environment, this will establish a sense of security for the child. This sense of security will provide the child with a safe base from which to explore the world with confidence and self-esteem. This allows the child to build a positive self-image and to expect positive reactions from other people around them throughout their lives.

Criticism for Bowlby's attachment theory is that he focused on the child's attachment to the mother, excluding other relationships. Further developments to Bowlby's attachment theory included Ainsworth's 'strange situation' experiment, which gave us the first piece of empirical evidence to prove Bowlby's theory (Ainsworth and Bell, 1970; Ainsworth et al, 1978). The strange situation procedure was carried out with children between the ages of one and two. It involved different stages that included:

- observing a child with her mother;
- letting a stranger join mother and child;
- letting the mother leave and the stranger stay;
- letting the mother return and the stranger leave;
- leaving the child entirely alone (Ainsworth and Bell, 1970).

Through her experiment Ainsworth identified three different types of attachment. The first type of attachment she named secure attachment. Secure attachment was evident in most of Ainsworth's sample of participant children. This is where the child is confident and secure that their caregiver will meet their needs. The infants felt they could explore and use the caregiver as a base. They also sought out their caregiver when they felt in distress. The other two types were insecure attachments, which she named 'insecure avoidant' and 'insecure ambivalent'. Insecure avoidant is where the infant does not gravitate back to their caregiver when exploring. They are independent from their caregiver both physically and emotionally. The caregiver is normally not emotionally available to them when they are in distress. The caregiver withdraws when help is needed with a challenging task.

Insecure ambivalent refers to the attachment style where the child will be clingy towards the caregiver. They do not take any comfort from the caregiver and therefore do not have the confidence to go and explore by themselves. They are difficult to soothe when they become upset as they are used to an inconsistent level of care from their caregiver. When the caregiver tries to interact with them they are likely to reject the caregiver's efforts.

Ainsworth's study was criticised (like all theory) on a number of points. One point that is very relevant to us is that she only 'tested' the attachment to the mother. What happens, for example, where a father raises his children or children stay with their grandparents? What is the impact on attachment then? Other researchers have found that these secure attachments relate not only to a mother but also to other caregivers as well, and that children can have a hierarchy of adults that they form attachments with (Main, 1999). According to Bowlby's attachment theory, children develop and learn best within a caring and supportive environment in which they have secure attachments. If children have insecure attachments this can have a negative impact on their social and emotional development throughout life.

Pause for thought and reflection

To what extent do you think the existence of caring and secure relationships in the home lives of children is needed for practitioners to develop positive, professional relationships with children and young people outside the home?

Do you think that practitioners can find value in the attachment theory of Bowlby and Ainsworth with regard to professional relationships with children and young people?

SUMMARY

This chapter has outlined key theories and concepts regarding child and adolescent development. In it we have introduced you to the following ideas:

- All theories have aspects that are good and positive about them but also some criticism.
- Piaget is a good starting point for looking at cognitive development.
- Vygotsky developed this further to include social learning and how children can learn more if they have help from adults or others who

know more than them. This difference between what they can learn by themselves and what they can achieve with the help of others is known as the 'zone of proximal development'.

- Behaviourists believe that children learn through cause and effect. The most well-known example of this is Pavlov's dogs. Pavlov conditioned the dogs' saliva reflex to take place when the dogs heard a buzzer rather than smelt food. This is known as 'classical conditioning'.
- Skinner, a behaviourist, found that if you reward behaviour it will happen again and if you punish behaviour it will act as a deterrent for this behaviour. This is known as 'operant conditioning'.
- Bandura's social learning theory demonstrates that children learn through observing the behaviour of others.
- Erikson developed the psychosocial development theory.
- Bowlby's attachment theory is a well-known theory about the importance of forming secure attachments during infancy.

FURTHER READING

One of the authors' all-time favourite books that provides a detailed description and unpacking of adolescence as a life stage and the biological, cognitive as well as identity formation that takes place during this time: Arnett, J.J. (2010) *Adolescence and emerging adulthood* (4th edn), London: Pearson.

An easy-to-follow and to-the-point book about human growth and development: Beckett, C. and Taylor, H. (2010) *Human growth and development*, London: Sage Publications.

A book that focuses on the way that very young babies and children learn and develop. It also goes beyond this to look at the policy implications for practice, effective leadership in settings and also developing appropriate relationships: Fabian, H. and Mould, C. (eds) (2009) *Development and learning for very young children*, London: Sage Publications.

ONLINE RESOURCES

To read more about the Ainsworth strange situation experiment and to view a video clip, visit the following website: www.simplypsychology. org/mary-ainsworth.html

A good way to make child development theory more 'real' to yourself is to watch video clips of the experiments that underpin the theories. We suggest that you search YouTube for video clips on Pavlov and classical conditioning and any other experiment or study that has caught your attention or that you are struggling to come to grips with: www.youtube.com

Another excellent resource for developing your understanding of child development through the viewing of video clips is: www.psychotube.net

5

key skills needed for practice

This chapter will introduce key skills that are needed by practitioners who work with children and young people. It is important to realise that we already started this process in Chapters Three and Four by introducing you to the social construction of childhood and youth and also child development. Having knowledge and understanding of these two areas are crucial skills for effective working. As will be seen in later chapters of this book, there is a wide range of practitioners who work with children and young people. We are aiming to introduce you here to a range of further skills that are crucial for all practitioners in this field of work.

Professionalism

This section will address key notions that underpin theories of professionalism. It will discuss personal values and professional ethics, including personal and professional boundaries that include creating a **work–life balance**. It will also explore reflective practice and the professional management of working practices, including planning, preparation, evaluation, time management and supervision. In this chapter we will refer to the children and young people who we work with as our clients. Another term that is used for them is **service users**.

Personal values and professional ethics

Personal values are a set of beliefs or principles that are used to guide a person into particular behaviours or actions. Values are a part of who we inherently are and how we relate to the world. Values are therefore part of our identity and will reflect how we see ourselves in relation to others (see Erikson's stages of psychosocial development in Chapter Four for more on identity formation). It is therefore easier to refer to values as particular to who we are.

Ethics are principles and rules of conduct within a professional environment. They are therefore moral rules that direct how we work with children and young people. Professional ethics are 'a set of ethical or moral principles that means something to people doing a particular type of job, usually as members of an occupation or professional group' (Banks, 2001, p 63). Some authors, like Banks (2001) herself, refer to these as professional values but in order to avoid confusion we will always refer to them as professional ethics.

The difference therefore is that personal values are individual and might not be shared by everyone in the same organisation or by people with similar roles. Professional ethics are shared by all members of a particular occupation. They therefore give practitioners guidelines such that they share the aims and principles of their organisation. When a situation arises where a practitioner's personal values might be at odds with the professional ethics of their organisation, professional ethics show the stance that their organisation would want them to take. Professional ethics can be set out by a professional body, for example the British Association of Social Workers (BASW) in the case of social work, and filtered down into the organisation's code of conduct. It can be set out in an organisation's mission statement and policies, for example in the case of the voluntary sector.

Personal and professional boundaries

Boundaries are about constraint; therefore they are about a practitioner stopping themselves from doing something that is outside of their remit or role. According to Ingram and Harris (2001), boundaries define what work you undertake and how you deliver the expected service, for example, what organisation you work for, who you work with, including colleagues in your own organisation but also partner organisations, your client group, the setting you work in and lastly when you work.

These boundaries are important to establish from a number of perspectives. Boundaries are important from the client's perspective as it leads to consistency in service provision from practitioners in similar roles. It provides the client with clarity with regard to what to expect from service providers and when to expect it. These boundaries are also a **safeguarding** tool as there should be clear boundaries with regard to personal and professional relationships between practitioners and their clients. A professional relationship is one that takes place within the boundaries of the job description and role of the practitioner. It is a working relationship that must adhere to professional ethics and must not step over into the personal life of the practitioner. In other words, it should not become a personal relationship between worker and client.

From the worker's perspective, boundaries are important as they will enable them to know where to draw the line with regard to tasks and responsibilities. It will enable them to know where their role begins and where it ends. This is important to ensure that practitioners do not duplicate work, in other words two or even more practitioners are working with the same client and using the same approach or programme. This might be good for the client but it can also lead to boredom, disengagement and also become costly for the organisation(s) delivering the service. Another scenario is that, without boundaries, a practitioner might undertake work that will undo or contradict work done by another practitioner. Within the caring professions practitioners feel under pressure (from external sources but also from themselves) to always be there for children and young people and to deliver when a need is identified (Ingram and Harris, 2001). If professional boundaries are in place then a practitioner has a chance at maintaining a work–life balance.

An example of a professional boundary would be the practice of not giving clients your personal mobile phone number and not meeting them outside your work hours or for social engagements. Sometimes you might need to agree additional hours with your line manager in order to meet the needs of a client but this will be agreed and monitored within the confines of a professional relationship. It is very important to ensure that you work within the professional boundaries of your role to protect both yourself and your clients. If you are at all unsure about possible boundaries, always ask your line manager, mentor or a co-worker.

Becoming a reflective practitioner

Part of being an effective practitioner is being a **reflective practitioner**, something we have already briefly presented to you in Chapter One. In Chapter One we introduced you to a reflective model by Gibbs (1988). As we have said previously, there is usually more than one theory or model for any concept or idea that we might discuss in this book. Another well-known model of the reflection process was developed by Boud et al (1985). This involves looking back at, actively thinking about and analysing what happened in practice and why a situation happened as it did. Boud et al's (1985) model also includes what the practitioner thought at the time and also how the practitioner felt about the situation.

In reflection the practitioner will think back to the experience. This will allow for a re-evaluation of the experience through thinking about why something went right or why something went wrong, attending to the feelings felt and what the practitioner can learn from them. This will allow for new perspectives on the situation that will enable the practitioner to think of alternative ways of dealing with a similar situation in future. The practitioner will then be ready to put these new perspectives into action when a similar situation arises (Boud et al, 1985). This model also encourages practitioners to reflect on experiences that others have had, ideas that practitioners have themselves or that others have shared and also the feelings of themselves or others with regard to a practice situation. This is valuable as it enables us to learn from others' experiences rather than having to make our own mistakes or to re-invent the wheel when someone else has some relevant insight to share.

Reflection is a continual cycle. It is not something that you do only as a beginner practitioner but constantly throughout your career. Your confidence will grow as a practitioner through reflection on your practice and linking theory with your practice. In the Further Reading section of this chapter, please look at the further models of reflection that are identified in Paige-Smith and Craft (2008).

Professional management process – planning, preparation, delivery and evaluation

The most visible part of working with children and young people is the physical one-to-one work or **group work** experiences. However, if you ask an experienced practitioner how many hours a week they spend on face-to-face work and how many hours they spend on tasks in preparation for the work, as well as evaluation and marking/assessing after the work, you might find the answer surprising.

Planning of a session, project or lesson is crucial in order to ensure that the work is focused on the children's learning, development or social needs. It is important to have children and young people's input when needs are identified. This will depend on the nature of the provision as well as the age and developmental stage of the children or young people. According to article 12 of the United Nations *Convention on the Rights of the Child* (UNCRC) (UN, 1989), children should have an input and have a voice with regard to decisions and services that impact on them.

Article 12 of the UNCRC

'1. States Parties shall assure to the child who is capable of forming his or her own views the right to express those views freely in all matters affecting the child, the views of the child being given due weight in accordance with the age and maturity of the child.

2. For this purpose the child shall in particular be provided the opportunity to be heard in any judicial and administrative proceedings affecting the child, either directly, or through a representative or appropriate body, in a manner consistent with the procedural rules of national law.'

The planning stage of a project or piece of work is the earliest stage to gain client involvement. No lower age limit is set for this client involvement. Younger children or children with specific difficulties are still able to express their views non-verbally. This can be through play, pictures and art, signing, the use of technology such as computers and whatever else might be needed. This may involve more creativity and input from you as the service provider but is crucial for making sure that *all* children and young people are treated fairly and have a say (Lansdown, 2001). We will address this further in Chapter Nine.

There are numerous planning tools and frameworks but here we will we will share with you the NAOMIE model of planning work with children and young people (Ingram and Harris, 2001). NAOMIE stands for:

Needs
Aims
Objectives
Methods
Implementation
Evaluation.

We suggest that when you have to plan a project or activity that you write down the letters that spell NAOMIE underneath each other like in the example below. This will help you to focus on and include all the necessary steps within your planning.

NAOMIE planning tool

N

A

O

M

I

E

It is important to realise that the first step to planning is to identify the needs of the client or client group, which should be carried out with their involvement as much as possible. When it comes to teaching the school **curriculum**, a teacher will not ask pupils what they want to learn but it might be appropriate to identify the learning styles of the pupils in order to ascertain the best teaching methods and styles for them.

The **aims** and **objectives** of the piece of work to address these needs form the second and third parts of the NAOMIE planning model.

How the work will be undertaken, in other words the **methods** used and what the project, lesson or session will look like, is the fourth part of the model. The fifth part of the model details **implementation** of the piece of work, which for some practitioners might be a lesson or an intervention and what resources are needed. Some practitioners might not have the time or space to work out all these aspects. Some are, for example, detached workers or meet with clients in a drop-in session and therefore they will react and provide an informed response on the spot. Having developed the key skill of reflection is crucial in these circumstances.

The final part of the model involves evaluation of the work. Evaluation and recording of work is important because these act as monitoring and assessment tools. They allow for a critical review of work (and are therefore also valuable tools in reflection and supervision). Recording of work after a practice session allows for the practitioner to 'take stock' so to speak of what was planned and what actually happened in the session and why. It also allows for clear action points to be identified that will then be incorporated in the planning of future sessions, lessons or interventions. Recording and evaluation therefore feed into planning and goal development for future sessions with children and young people (see Figure 5.1).

Figure 5.1: The cyclical nature of planning and evaluation

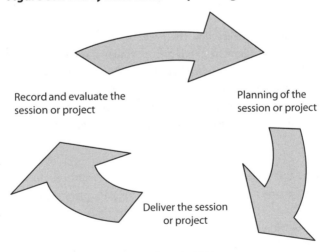

Record and evaluate the
session or project

Planning of the
session or project

Deliver the session
or project

Source: Adapted from Ingram and Harris, 2001

Recording and evaluation after a session are also a way of providing evidence of work undertaken. In a policy environment where it is needed to justify expenses and where there is competition for resources, recording and evaluation are key to explaining the value of the service you deliver and also to make a case for sustained use of resources. Recording and evaluation are therefore a valuable way to illustrate **accountability**.

Please remember that there are a number of different planning tools and it is best to use the one that your organisation prefers. However, all these tools draw on similar notions in order to ensure that your sessions or lessons are fit for purpose. Another easy-to-use planning tool is the questions framework. This can be used for planning a long-term project or for on-the-spot planning. With this tool, work is planned using the six simple questions of 'what?', 'why?', 'when?', 'how?', 'where?' and 'who?', immortalised by Rudyard Kipling in the following poem.

The elephant's child

I keep six honest serving-men
(They taught me all I knew);
Their names are What and Why and When
And How and Where and Who.

(Kipling, 1902)

Time management

A key skill needed to be an effective practitioner is management of the self. This links with clear personal and professional boundaries but also knowing the difference between your personal values and the professional ethics of your organisation. Time management is key in the caring professions as our personal values might set the agenda as this may have provided the driving force for why we got involved in working in this field in the first place. This can therefore lead us to undertake tasks driven by our personal values rather than the professional ethics that underpin our job role and responsibilities. Our personal values are what makes us respond to requests to put on more provision and run more sessions or lessons. We feel that if we do not do it the children or young people will miss out. In practice there are numerous demands on our time and it is important to be able to manage and prioritise these demands so as not to be overwhelmed by competing demands. Ingram and Harris (2001) appropriately named this the 'kipper effect'. The 'kipper effect' creates a mental picture of a fish representing workers that have too many demands on their time and due to them saying yes to everything they become to resemble a kipper fish, which is flat and has eyes that looks in different directions! Therefore a worker will become ineffective and overwhelmed as they will be unable to effectively complete tasks. This will lead to feelings of dissatisfaction, stress, overwork and ultimately ineffectiveness. Work–life balance will be impossible to maintain and this can create problems in a worker's personal life as well.

Pause for thought and reflection

Make a list of all the demands on your time on a typical day.

After you have done this, think about how you approach these demands. Do you approach each situation and demand as they come up or do you have a system to get through your tasks every day?

It can be useful to undertake a time audit. Look at how many hours you will work over a particular time period. Then look at what projects, lessons or interventions you are working on within this time period. Work out the time that you are expected to work on each of these sessions, cases or projects. This will provide you with information about whether you have too many work commitments and cases for your work hours or too few. If you have been in practice for a few years you can also look at what you had to do in a typical previous month and whether the tasks and hours matched up or whether you had a deficit or surplus of time.

There are also a number of time-wasting activities that we engage in every day. It is important to identify these and to respond appropriately to them. These could be, for example, spending too much time on e-mails, interaction on social network sites, procrastinating when writing reports, coffee and tea breaks with co-workers and so on. Examples here can be endless, but it is important to identify real time-wasting activities rather than targeting the wrong activities. We are not saying that there isn't value in these activities in themselves for you and your work; what we are saying is that it is only when you start spending too much time on them that they become a problem.

Pause for thought and reflection

Do you think spending time throughout the day talking to your co-workers and members from other organisations is a time-wasting activity or an appropriate networking and information-sharing opportunity?

Supervision

An eminent writer on the subject of supervision, Kadushin (1992) states that supervision has three main functions or areas of interest: administrative, educational and supportive supervision. According to McGillivray and Davies (2010), the role of a supervisor is crucial in providing the practitioner with the opportunity to reflect back on experiences that they have had in the workplace. This should be a focus not only on what went wrong but very importantly also on what went right and why it went wrong or right. Can you see the link with being a reflective practitioner here? Supervision can take place within a one-to-one meeting or within a group context (Kadushin and Harkness, 2002). Within a group supervision context, it is more difficult to address individual needs of practitioners. Therefore it is a good idea to undertake group as well as individual supervision. As seen later in this chapter, supervision should aim to provide a worker with a safe space to share emotions and feelings, especially after dealing with difficult situations. This will allow the worker to deal with these feelings but also to avoid burn-out. The supervisor is normally a more senior worker or line manager whose role is to keep the focus on the supervisee and their work. The key skills identified in the next section of this chapter are crucial to a good supervisor–supervisee relationship, which explores what the worker already knows and does well, but also discovers and explores new thoughts and interpretations of actions and events. The supervisor should be a sounding board for the supervisee.

It is easy for a supervisor–supervisee relationship to turn into one where the supervisor is seen as the expert and the supervisee becomes dependent on this person to clarify and offer solutions when needed. A more helpful and developmental approach is to follow the solution-focused approach to supervision. The starting point for this approach is that the supervisee already has solutions and ideas or the ability to generate these for their own concerns or developmental areas in their practice. Supervision therefore should be an enabling or empowering process, whereby the skills and power lie with the supervisee to bring about change and develop both themselves and their practice.

Connecting with children and young people

This section identifies and examines the key skills and competences utilised by practitioners when working with children and young people. The same basic key skills will be needed whether you are working with an individual or a group. However, the levels of intensity, the number of aspects you have to focus on as well as the needs of your clients might differ.

Verbal and non-verbal communication

In our experience, the most important skill in working with children and young people is communication: 'Good communication is central to working with children, young people, their families and carers.... It involves listening, questioning, understanding and responding to what is being communicated by children, young people and those caring for them' (DfES, 2005, p 6). But what do we mean when we refer to communication with children and young people?

Pause for thought and reflection

When you read the words verbal and non-verbal communication, what do you think of?

In working with children and young people it is important to realise the full extent of what is meant by these two different categories of communication. This will become more apparent in the further chapters on working within early years and also working with children.

Verbal communication

Verbal communication is the sharing of information through spoken words and sounds in a shared language. The aim of communication is to transfer knowledge and information, in other words a message, from a person who is sending a message (sender) to a person or group of people who are receiving the message (receiver). The message must be encoded by the sender to make it understandable and decoded by the receiver. This is known as the communication process (Lefevre, 2010).

A number of factors can hinder the message reaching the recipient in the way it was intended or can stop the message reaching the recipient at all! Noise, for example, will make it difficult for the recipient to hear the message or it could result in the message only being heard partly, leading to misunderstanding. This is the reality of a variety of practice settings/environments that we introduce you to in Part Two of this book. In a youth club or playwork environment, for example, noise and boisterous activity can be a reality of the nature of the work. We are not saying that all settings should be quiet but rather that the impact of noise on communication should be considered. This could be done by moving to a quieter corner, adapting the volume of your voice or reading the social cues to ensure that the child or young person is able to hear you. Crucially, admit when you can't fully hear what others are saying to you. This sounds obvious but think about the number of times you are sitting there nodding away at someone talking to you with not a clue what they are really saying because of noise! We know, this happens to us as well! Communication can also be impacted on by the recipient not paying attention as they were not expecting communication to take place or because of environmental or emotional distractions or disruptions. As a practitioner it is therefore important to read the situation and to bear in mind the environment to ensure that both the physical and also emotional environment are conducive to effective communication.

Clarity of the message is crucial for effective communication. The message should be delivered in a clear voice but also in understandable and accessible language. This would be determined by the stage of development and age of the child or young person in question. It is important not to alienate the child through language and communication that is too difficult and complex but also not to patronise the child or young person with language that is too simplistic. It is also important to incorporate visual aids and other alternative methods of communication to ensure clarity of message, for example by using pictures or diagrams and actions that reinforce the message communicated. With children who might be hard of hearing or deaf, sign language, for example Makaton, British Sign Language or American Sign Language, is necessary as well as the above-mentioned visual aids as and when appropriate. For blind children, Braille reading material might be used to act as a reminder or to add an extra dimension to the message shared. This is all part of encoding the message.

The child or young person needs to decode the message after receiving it. They will then provide you with feedback. This feedback might take the form of a verbal response that can clearly show you that they understood or misunderstood the meaning of what you tried to convey. The feedback can also take the form of a sigh or other non-verbal communication; even a blank stare! Based on the feedback you receive from the child or young person, you will be able to clarify the message if needed.

Figure 5.2 provides a pictorial representation of the communication process.

Figure 5.2: The communication process

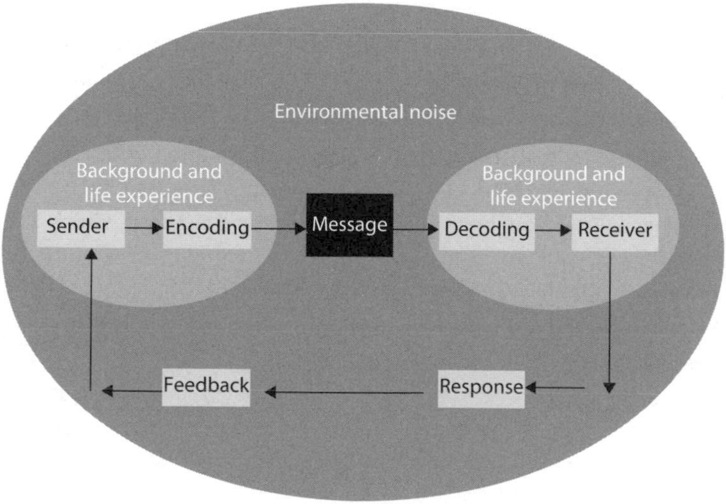

Source: Adapted from Lefevre, 2010

Non-verbal communication

Non-verbal communication involves the sharing of messages through means other than with spoken words. The most well-known aspect of non-verbal communication is body language. This includes aspects such as posture, facial expression, gestures and also how and where you position your body in relation to the person you are communicating with.

Non-verbal communication also refers to paralanguage – the non-verbal elements in speech – for example the tone of voice, rhythm of speech, emotion in voice, speaking style and also accent. Accent, for example, can make the simplest message completely alien. Therefore, as workers we need to be aware of our accents, how fast or slow we speak, our pitch and other factors as all these impact on the effectiveness and clarity of our communication. Being aware of these aspects in ourselves will enable us to communicate in an anti-oppressive manner with young people (we discuss anti-oppressive practice in more detail in Chapter Nine).

Research has found that when verbal and non-verbal communication convey different meanings or messages, the recipient of the message will believe the non-verbal cues (Giannini et al, 1993). For example, if a young person shares some disturbing information with you and you respond with 'thank you for telling me, let's see what we can do together to help you' but your facial expression registers shock and disbelief and your voice is panicked, the young person is going to remember and believe these non-verbal messages. This could lead to the young person not trusting you any more and set back the working relationship that you have developed with them.

Listening

A crucial part of communication in the working relationship is listening. In recent years the focus has been on active listening. Active listening is a process developed by Carl Rogers (1983) and involves two important aspects: listener orientation and reflective technique. Listener orientation involves congruence, unconditional positive regard and empathic understanding. Let's look at each of these in turn.

Listener orientation involves the basic skills needed in order to work successfully with a child or young person. Rogers generally wrote for people engaged in counsellor situations. However, he was also an educationalist and his person-centred approach is relevant for an understanding of skills needed to work effectively with children and young people in a variety of settings.

Congruence means to be real and genuine in interactions with others. It is important to not put on a façade but for workers to be themselves. A worker who tries to hide who they really are, their feelings and personality will allow more scope to be ineffective in their interactions with children and young people. However, it is crucial to remember what we covered earlier in this chapter with regard to personal and professional boundaries and to ensure that what you do portray is to the child's benefit and not yours and also within your professional boundaries and ethics.

The second of these core conditions is unconditional positive regard. This is also known as non-possessive warmth and relates to an understanding that the child or young person is a human being and that they have worth in their own right and should be respected. In practice this will equate to the understanding that when working with challenging young people we can dislike the behaviour and challenge the behaviour but we do not dislike the young person. This will put children and young people at ease to realise that nothing that they can tell a practitioner will influence the worker negatively towards them as a person. This also means that we will make a distinction between the behaviour and a child/young person. Therefore we will not say 'you are a naughty child' but rather say 'your behaviour is unacceptable'. This is intended to ensure that workers do not act on preconceptions, stereotypes or judgements concerning a child or young person. This is also linked to Becker's (1963) labelling theory. Labelling theory relates to the idea that people can be stereotyped and that others then attach a 'label' to the person that relates to the stereotype, for example the 'naughty child', the 'sensitive child' or 'the troubled youth'. At times, practitioners and others are more likely to see the label rather than the individual child or young person. Children and young people are used to people not listening to them or trying to mould and discipline them when they don't act in the expected and accepted manner. Children and young people specifically will try to push these boundaries and will try to get a reaction out of a practitioner in order to see whether the worker will still be there for them and want to work with them. They are trying to determine whether they can trust the worker or not. More on this in Chapter Nine.

The third core condition refers to having an empathic understanding for the situation of the child or young person. Empathic understanding is different from sympathy. Empathy means that the practitioner is aiming to understand how the child or young person is feeling from the child/young person's perspective, therefore putting themselves into the child/young person's shoes (Rogers, 1983).

The second element of active listening is reflective technique. This involves reflecting and rephrasing the message that the child or young person has shared with the practitioner back to the child. It is a technique to ensure that what the practitioner heard is the message that the child or young person tried to convey. It is also a way of clarifying the message that was received. Reflection also has more than one outcome; it shows the child or young person that the practitioner is paying attention to them. This can be achieved through both verbal and non-verbal affirmation.

It is very important to bear in mind cultural differences when working with children and young people. Nodding or shaking of a head, as well as making or maintaining eye contact, can have different meanings in different cultures. A practitioner might endeavour to display that they are giving the child their undivided attention by trying to maintain eye contact but this can have a negative impact if, for example, cultural differences are not acknowledged. Reflection can also provide encouragement to the child or young person to continue to share and discuss. This can take the form of a nod, a little smile, or the practitioner can paraphrase or repeat back the last sentences to the young person in order to maintain the sharing of information. The practitioner can also use silence, or an open-ended question, to try to stimulate the flow of conversation.

We could write a whole book on the importance of effective communication with children, young people and their families. Unfortunately, we do not have the space here but look in the Further Reading section of this chapter for good books that we identified for you with regard to communication, which includes Egan's *The skilled helper*, which is a very effective tool.

Safeguarding and protecting children and young people

The role of practitioners in keeping children and young people safe will be examined in this section. The notions underpinning safeguarding policies and practice will be identified and the important role of practitioners will be discussed.

Internationally, countries that ratified the United Nations *Convention on the Rights of the Child* (UNCRC) (UN, 1989) have agreed that 'children should be protected from abuse and neglect' (UNCRC, article 19). Once a country ratifies the UNCRC, the expectation is that it will adopt the articles of the convention into its national legislation. Like many other western countries, the UK has a state-regulated system for the protection of children and young people. The legislation that underpins the child protection and safeguarding practices within the UK are the Children Act 1989 and the subsequent Children Act 2004.

Children Act 1989

The Children Act 1989 differentiates between 'children in need' and children 'at risk of significant harm'.

'Children in need' are covered in section 17 of the Children Act 1989. The term refers to children and families that will need to make use of additional support and services in order to safeguard and promote their welfare.

Under section 47 of the Children Act 1989, the relevant local authority is under a duty to make enquiries where it has reasonable cause to suspect that a child is suffering or likely to suffer significant harm. Crucially, you do not have to have proof that a child is suffering significant harm under one of the categories of abuse but a reasonable cause to suspect triggers these duties. This is in order to safeguard children and to ensure that, no matter who the practitioners involved are, all children will have the same likelihood of being protected.

What do we mean by significant harm? Section 31 of the Children Act 1989 defines 'harm' as 'ill-treatment or the impairment of health or development'. 'Development' refers to the physical, intellectual, emotional, social or behavioural development of a child. 'Health' implies both physical and mental health. 'Ill-treatment' includes sexual abuse and forms of ill-treatment that are not physical.

Of cardinal importance is the fact that 'significant' is not defined because what may constitute significant harm for one child may not for another. A professional judgement is required in each individual situation. Therefore the skills and knowledge that each individual practitioner possesses are of crucial importance in child protection.

So what are the skills needed to determine whether a child is in need of additional support services or whether a child is being abused? A certain amount of knowledge is needed in order to identify the needs of children and young people with regard to child protection. Practitioners have to have knowledge concerning the different categories of abuse in order to ascertain whether a child is being abused or not. They also need to have knowledge and an understanding of their duties that are triggered when identifying 'children in need' or children 'at risk of significant harm'. All practitioners have a duty to safeguard children and young people. One of the practitioners in a related role is the family support worker.

Pen picture – Tamara

As a family support worker, you work very closely on a continuous basis with families associated with social services for reasons that may be related to concerns with the parents' history, poor parenting or family issues that may affect the child's physical or emotional state. Many problems that these families face could be a history of drug abuse, being a victim of sexual or physical abuse, mental health issues, neglectful parenting and many more, which means their child is identified as a child in need or is placed on the child protection register as a result. I work in a Child Protection Unit where up to nine families live for a minimum of three months, and are under 24-hour observation and supervision to assess whether they can meet the needs of their child/children in the community once their assessment is complete. Family support workers observe how these families can parent and care for their child in various scenarios, and at the end of their assessment, such observations will work towards a decision of whether the child will be removed from the parents into foster care/adoption, or remain with the parents in the community or within further support services as necessary for their needs. Family support workers tend to be trusted by clients more so than a social worker or manager as they are not viewed as 'the enemy', but rather as a support mechanism. Family support workers, however, prove to be the eyes and ears of social services, as all evidence of a family's parenting abilities are primarily identified through us.

An understanding and knowledge of the processes followed in your individual country and organisation are needed. If you are working in any capacity with children and young people, make an appointment with your line manager to discuss your organisation's child protection policy and procedures to follow if you suspect a child is being abused or that a child might need additional support.

There are four different categories of abuse that are adhered to within the UK and also in some other countries. These are physical abuse, sexual abuse, emotional abuse and neglect. They are defined in the *Working together to safeguard children* documentation (DH, 1999, 2006; see also the Children Act 2010). All the categories of abuse constitute maltreatment of a child. They all involve inflicting harm to a child or someone neglecting to stop harm happening to a child (DCSF, 2010).

The definitions for the different categories of abuse are very detailed and thorough so as to provide practitioners with clarity. To see these definitions in full for the UK, visit the Department for Education website (www.education.gov.uk) and download the document *Working together to safeguard children* (DCSF, 2010).

The categories of abuse have signs and symptoms that can indicate that a child is being abused or neglected. Some of the signs and a lot of the symptoms are similar, therefore observation is a key skill needed in identifying child protection concerns in order to deal with them appropriately. All children and young people are unique and every situation is different. Before a practitioner can do anything to support a child being abused it is important to recognise that abuse is taking place in the first place. This can happen in a variety of different ways:

- observing the signs and symptoms of abuse (DCSF, 2010);
- observing the abuse taking place;
- being told by a child or young person that they are being abused – this is called disclosure. In early years settings where a child is unable to fully speak or might not understand what is happening to them, this 'telling' or 'disclosure' can take the form of acting out scenarios or feelings through play (for more on the importance of play, see Chapter Six). This can also happen through the creative expression of drawings, paintings or moulding play clay;

■ being told by someone else who either observed it or heard about it from the child or young person in question or someone else.

Observation

Observation involves a practitioner not only seeing the physical signs of abuse but also observing changes in behaviour and levels of engagement. Careful observation will provide a practitioner with non-verbal information as well as potentially verbal information. This will enable them to identify changes that are taking place within the child. For example, a pre-adolescent child used to be friendly, outgoing and engaged but over the last few weeks he has become quiet and closed, appears to be nervous and worried as he is biting his nails and fidgeting (he did not do this previously) and he is wearing a sweater even though it is hot outside. This will provide the practitioner with information that there has been a change in the child's emotional state that might indicate that abuse may be a concern.

Practitioners should be able to add this visual information to other information that they might have received through verbal and/or non-verbal communication. They might have received this other information from the child or young person themselves, from the child's friends, family members or from other practitioners.

Handling disclosure

This leads us to the skills needed to effectively deal with a disclosure without inflicting a form of 'secondary victimisation' on a child or young person. Disclosures are when a child or young person tells you themselves that they are concerned about their safety and welfare. They are telling you that something is happening to them (or to others) that they want to stop. Depending on the age and developmental maturity of the child, the way of disclosure (be it verbally or through play) as well as the setting will differ.

When a child or young person discloses information about abuse to you, it is crucial to listen to them. You must portray a willingness to take what they say seriously. In the past, when children and young people have shared stories of abuse they have not always been believed. A perception that children in care or looked-after children could not be trusted contributed to the perpetuation of abuse in care institutions in the 20th century (Waterhouse, 2000). In recent times there has been a greater emphasis on listening to children. This is mostly as a result of the UNCRC, which advocated a participatory rights-based approach. This means that children and young people should have a voice in aspects that concern them. The Children Act 1989, the Every Child Matters agenda, the Children Act 2004 as well as the 'Learning to Listen' framework (CYPU, 2001), ensured that this international agenda made its way into national legislation and practice in the UK.

It is important that you remain calm, attentive and reassuring as well as non-judgemental. This includes not making any assumptions or judgements concerning the child or young person disclosing the information but also not making assumptions about the person who is abusing them. The abuser can be a beloved parent or carer whom the child loves and they may already be feeling disloyal and conflicted about sharing the abuse.

It is a skill to be able to effectively deal with hearing heart-wrenching and sometimes also quite shocking disclosures from children and young people. It is important to work through possible feelings before you find yourself in this type of situation as this is not the place to look shocked or to break down yourself. This is where reflection on practice through case studies and examples shared by other practitioners, as well as training and supervision, can be useful. Think back to what you learned earlier in this chapter in the section on connecting with children and young people. If what you are verbally communicating and what you are non-verbally communicating are at odds with each other then the recipient will remember the non-verbal messages. Therefore, use positive body language and appear to have time and portray the competence to deal with the disclosure and the needs of the child or young person involved. As practitioners ourselves we feel strongly that everyone can do this through focusing on the positive. You are making a difference to a child's life and helping them to move forward. We suggest that it is crucial for practitioners to receive supervision after dealing with a disclosure or any other way of finding out about a child protection concern. This is important for debriefing, morale and support, in line with the supportive function of supervision.

As we have seen, communication is key in dealing with a disclosure. The messages that a practitioner conveys and how they do this will be crucial in whether the child or young person continues the disclosure or stops even before they start sharing. Therefore, as soon as it becomes clear that a child or young person is going to verbally disclose, remind them that you can't keep the information secret, but that you will have to pass it on in order for them to receive help and support. Communicate to the child that they are right to tell and that they are doing the correct thing by telling you. Make sure that you inform the child about what will happen next and that they will have to tell their story to someone else as well. As far as possible, allow the child to be supported by the person that they choose to disclose to, as the child perhaps feels that they can trust a particular person better. Remember that if this is you, the child has chosen you for a particular reason and because they think that you can help them. This does not mean that you would interview them or talk to their parents but that you will be around to provide support for the child through the process that needs to be followed.

Collaborative working and information sharing

The last key skill that this chapter will discuss is working together in order to provide children and young people with the best possible service. Effective working together will allow for information sharing in order to build up a comprehensive picture of the child or young person's reality. This will enable practitioners to not only identify children and young people's needs but also to develop a corresponding plan of action that will be both achievable and effective. The same core skills needed to work effectively with children and young people are the skills needed to work effectively with other organisations. These are, for example, communication, personal and professional boundaries, professional ethics, time management and an understanding of child protection and **safer working practices**.

It is also a skill to know what information to share, what information not to share and who to share it with. Information sharing does not provide us with the right to tell everyone about a client's concerns – only the people that they are relevant to. The skill is for you to work out whether sharing certain information will add to and enhance a client's service provision and life experience or not. Structures, policies and guidance will be in place to enable a practitioner to do this; however, the skills identified in this chapter will aid this process.

This chapter was very much a whistle-stop tour of some of the further key skills needed to effectively work with children and young people. Please do see this as a starting point to consider the skills you will need rather than an exhaustive and detailed exploration.

SUMMARY OF KEY POINTS

This chapter has identified the further key skills needed to work effectively with children and young people. These skills are:

- the ability to act with professionalism – this includes maintaining personal values and professional ethics, maintaining personal and professional boundaries, being a reflective practitioner who plans their work and manages their time and also undergoing supervision;
- the ability to professionally connect with children and young people – this involves verbal and non-verbal communication through a person-centred approach that includes active listening, listener orientation and reflective technique;
- the crucial skill of safeguarding and protecting children and young people through listening, observation and the ability to effectively and sensitively handle disclosures;

■ the importance of collaborative working and appropriate information sharing.

FURTHER READING

A good introductory text to communication skills and the importance of effective communication with children and their families: Dunhill, A., Elliot, B. and Shaw, A. (eds) (2009) *Effective communication and engagement with children and young people, their families and carers*, Exeter: Learning Matters.

The book that we refer you to in the section on communication skills: Egan, G. (2009) *The skilled helper: A problem-management and opportunity-development approach to helping* (9th edn), Belmont, CA: Wadsworth.

A book with a focus on communication with children as well as how to develop appropriate working relationships with children. It goes on to look at children's participation in service delivery as well as looking at practice relationships. The book ends with discussion of the very important role of helping children to deal with **transitions**: Foley, P. and Leverett, S. (2008) *Connecting with children: Developing working relationships*, Bristol: The Policy Press.

An excellent and comprehensive book on effective communication with children and young people. It sheds light on not only the experiences and expectations of social workers with regard to communication skills but also what children and young people say about their social workers: Lefevre, M. (2010) *Communicating with children and young people: Making a difference*, Bristol: The Policy Press.

A book that is written specifically for youth workers but is a valuable source for all practitioners working with children and young people with regard to professional ethics and personal values: Roberts, J. (2009) *Youth work ethics*, Exeter: Learning Matters.

A book that introduces further models of reflection but also roots it in early years practice: Paige-Smith, A. and Craft, A. (eds) (2008) *Developing reflective practice in the early years*, Maidenhead: Open University Press.

ONLINE RESOURCES

NSPCC: https://www.nspcc.org.uk/

ThinkUKnow: www.thinkuknow.co.uk/

If you want to find out more about the different learning styles, we suggest that those developed by Honey and Mumford are a good place to start: www.peterhoney.com/content/tools-learningstyles.html

6

working with the early years (from birth to age five)

In this chapter we will explore and examine the key theories and themes that underpin working with the early years specifically. We will also describe and consider the various approaches to working with infants, toddlers and children from birth to age five and explore the issues that are specific to this age group.

The importance of the early years

As described in Chapter Three, the early years can be seen as a separate life and development stage. It is normally seen as the stage in life before a child enters formal, mandatory education. Please note that we do not use the term 'schooling' here but rather 'education', as some families opt for alternative means to provide mandatory education, for example, home-schooling their children. As will be seen in Chapter Seven, school starting age is different in different countries due to the social construction of childhood. However, for the purposes of this book we will focus on early years provision as provision for infants, toddlers and children from birth to age five.

This stage is also part of what is known as early childhood. Early childhood incorporates the infant stage, toddlerhood and preschool stage as well as children between the ages of six and eight years.

.

As seen in Chapter Four, early childhood is a period of great physical, cognitive as well as social development and growth. In line with this we therefore agree with Field (2010b) that good-quality input is necessary during this life stage. If we look back at Chapter Four and Erikson's (1968) stages of psychosocial development, it is clear that, according to Erikson, parents are the source of the most significant relationships at this age. This also links with Bowlby's (1969) attachment theory and Bandura's (1977) social learning theory. Parents, as early socialisation examples, are children's first educators and role models. What happens in cases where parents are not in the best position to adequately support their children in these early years?

Pause for thought and reflection

Where parents are unable to provide the level of care and support needed in the early years, do you think that the government has any responsibility to help or should families help themselves? Jot down your initial thoughts on this.

Your thoughts on this might change or stay the same through reading this chapter. The chapter will give you more information based on research studies in order to develop your thoughts and opinion into a reasoned argument.

Before we start addressing working with the early years, we would like to set the context for you. There are different sectors that people can work in within Britain. It is important to have an understanding of these sectors as this impacts on the practitioners that we are identifying in the following four chapters.

Who works with children and young people?

There are three sectors (Directgov, 2011b) within public society in Britain: the public, the private and the voluntary and community sectors (the last of these is also known as the 'not-for-profit' or 'third' sector). It is important to know about these different sectors because if you choose to work with children and young people you will work in one of these areas. At this stage you may be considering a career in this field. You should consider what type of work you would like to do and which type of organisation you would like to work for as this may well support you to more effectively choose the right career, and any professional development that may be necessary. As we briefly identified in the opening chapter, your employer will affect the work you do as well as the terms and conditions of this employment, that is, your working hours, the number of days' holidays and the values that underpin the work. In reality, though, the likelihood is that your agency will need to work with a range of professionals and agencies, which may be situated in the other sectors. It is extremely useful to understand the perspectives, aims and objectives of the other organisations working in your area. It will also be useful if you are looking for alternative employment.

The **public sector** is owned and run by the government. Within England, you will usually find two tiers locally: a county council and district council. County councils cover large geographical areas and are responsible for providing most public services. This includes schools, social services and public transport. Each county is divided into smaller areas called districts (also known as boroughs or cities depending on the area covered). District councils are responsible for providing services such as gyms and leisure facilities, local planning and council housing as well as recycling and rubbish collection (Directgov, 2011b).

You may also find unitary authorities in England and Wales. This is where there is only one level of government and may be in a large town, a city (for example Peterborough), a small county (for example Rutland and Powys) or the London boroughs.

In Scotland there is only one level of government – council areas – and therefore it is a unitary system. In Northern Ireland there are borough, city and district councils (NI Direct, 2010). It is important to note that in Northern Ireland these councils have different responsibilities from councils in other areas of the UK.

Within the public sector, there are also town and parish councils, called 'community councils' in Scotland and Wales. Northern Ireland doesn't have an equivalent. These cover quite a small area. They have responsibility for areas of public life such as allotments, local halls and community centres, parks and ponds, public toilets and war memorials. These organisations are sometimes referred to as the 'third tier' of government (Directgov, 2011b).

The public sector is a major employer for professionals working with children and young people. You may well be working for or with a public sector organisation if you are an education welfare officer, a teacher, a social worker or a youth worker.

The **private sector** is the part of the country's economy that is not owned or controlled by the government. Organisations within the private sector are set up to make their owners and shareholders money. In recent years there has been a growth in private providers of services for young people. You will find private companies delivering holiday schemes and projects, out-of-school clubs as well as children's homes and alternative education.

Finally, there is the voluntary and community sector. It is important to note that this title fails to really take into account the varied organisation types that you might find in the sector such as social enterprises. This is because the **third sector** generally covers all other areas not covered or run by the state (government) in the public sector, or the private sector.

Who works with the early years?

Whatever age range or life stage you are interested in working with, it is important to remember that the full age spectrum and every stage of childhood is relevant. This is because the individual you might work with is not just the person you see in front of you. We are all a result of our environment, our experiences and our influences. In short, we are all the sum of everything that we experience from birth and indeed from conception. Children and young people bring all of this with them when we work with them. A holistic and complete understanding of childhood is therefore necessary to be an effective and empathic worker with children and young people.

The tasks you might become involved in as someone working within early years and early childhood are extremely varied. According to the Children's Workforce Development Council (CWDC) (from April 2012 this was replaced by the Teaching Agency), working in early years can see you involved in the daily care and welfare of babies and small children. Depending on the age range you work with, this could include changing nappies, feeding, bathing and dressing children. You may be involved in helping children to develop certain skills, for example toilet training, feeding and dressing themselves. Health and safety as well as safeguarding will be important parts of any role in the field. You will be involved in the encouragement and development of young children's social and emotional development. You will be involved in helping young children to explore the world around them and be a crucial part in their early experiences of literacy and numeracy. Outdoor and indoor play should be encouraged and supported. Communication with parents will be crucial for you in order to work with each other to the benefit of the child's development. As with all roles within the field, partnership working is key in order to ensure that the child has the best opportunities, care and support. Other practitioners you might work with are health or social care providers, for example health visitors, general practitioners, speech therapists and social workers (CWDC, 2011).

Where you might work with the early childhood age range

You can work with a child during their early childhood in a variety of different settings in a variety of different roles. You can work with a child within their own home (as a nanny or au pair), within your house (as a childminder), at a church hall, at a village hall or at any other suitable venue (at a **nursery** or **preschool**), or attached to a school (nursery or preschool). You might also work in a **Sure Start**

children's centre, **community centre** or for a private **day-care provider** in a nursery. These settings relate to the physical space or places that you might work with young children.

You will work with young children with regard to where they are at developmentally. For example, you might work with a child with speech delay (speech and language therapist), a child with emotional problems (educational psychologist or counsellor) or you might be involved with them and their family to help with emotional or physical issues that might put them at risk of significant harm (social worker). Another service is to provide support for a family when they are going through a difficult period (family support worker).

With the change in parental working patterns due to government policy and economic pressures, demand for early years care has risen significantly. This includes earlier starting times and later pick-ups. The aim of this chapter is not to debate the impact of early childcare on children but rather to introduce you to the job opportunities available to you within this field.

Pause for thought and reflection

Do you know any one, either in a personal or professional capacity, who works with children during early childhood? What is their job role? What type of work do they do? Who do they work for? If you are not sure of the answers to any of these questions, why not ask to talk to them about their work?

You do not have to do this exercise, but it might help you if you are thinking about a future career working with children during early childhood. You will already have started your list of people to contact to discuss volunteering with or for advice.

As we have previously stated, there are a number of different roles for practitioners and professionals within the different sectors.

Practitioners and professionals are predominantly found working within the public or voluntary and community sectors. They include childminders, nursery assistants, social workers, parent support advisers and nannies or au pairs (private sector). As we identified in Chapter Two, there have been a number of policy changes that have affected those working with children and young people since 1997. With each different policy change and refocus, practitioners have often found their work realigned to fit new government policy. In the early years sector, the biggest change has been the introduction of the Early Years Foundation Stage (EYFS) (see the next subsection) for settings working with children under the age of five, and there are now new changes following the Tickell Review (Tickell, 2011). This has had a significant impact on the workforce (for example, a reduction in the number of learning goals that a child is assessed in by age five from 69 to 17. Further developments include a reduction in form filling and bureaucracy and more focus on spending time with the children, as well as more feedback to parents concerning their child's development. However, the core professional ethics and some of the main roles of practitioners remain predominantly unchanged. The personal values that drive someone like you to express an interest in working with children in early childhood will also still remain the same. For example you may want to make a difference to families by providing support to them and their young children in a variety of settings and circumstances. Alternatively you might want to be an early educator or role model for young children. Providing care and support for babies, wanting to make a difference in your community or society in general, is an equally valid motivating factor. Whatever your personal reasons for expressing an interest in this field, we hope that you find this introduction to some of the main professions working with young children valuable.

Before we go on to introduce you to some work roles available with this stage of childhood, we will address the early years curriculum. This is a UK policy initiative that changed the face of early years provision significantly across the different sectors (public, private and voluntary). Research undertaken by the Effective Provision of Pre-school Education (EPPE) project (Sylva et al, 2004) shows that participation in early years education from the age of two onwards can lead to better outcomes

– both educationally and socially. It also suggests that early years education (preschool) that is part time or full time and of all levels of quality has positive effects on a child's development compared to children who do not access early years education.

Early years curriculum

Most countries do not have national curriculum guidelines for children under the age of five. Some people feel that a curriculum for infants, toddlers and children from birth to age five is a good idea while others feel that it is not a good idea as children all have very different life experiences in this age range. This early years curriculum has been dubbed the 'nappy curriculum'.

Pause for thought and reflection

What do you think about a curriculum for infants, toddlers and children from birth to age five?

Do you think that it is an idea with some merit or not?

What are you basing your thoughts on?

Do you think that some children might benefit from a curriculum at this age?

In England, the early years curriculum spans from the ages of nought to five. This is called the Early Years Foundation Stage (EYFS) and was introduced and made statutory in September 2008. All schools and early years providers, for example childminders, day nurseries, reception and nursery classes (preschool) in state or independent schools, playgroups, after-school and breakfast clubs, holiday provision as well as Sure Start children's centres, have to follow this to some degree. Some of these settings will have to follow the whole EYFS while others will only have to follow the parts that are relevant for their setting and the nature of their role. Mother and toddler groups, nannies, au pairs, as well as other short-term childcare provision such as crèches at gyms, do not have to adhere to the EYFS.

The EYFS built on and brought together three different sets of guidance and frameworks for service provision within the early years. This includes the *Curriculum guidelines for the foundation stage* (2000), *Birth to three matters* (2002) and the *National standards for the under-8s daycare and childminding* (2003) (national strategy website, cited in Beckley et al, 2009, p 2). Since 1 September 2012, a revised EYFS has been followed. At the time of the introduction of the original EYFS, it was made clear that a review of it would take place to identify the value of the curriculum. Practitioners and parents were asked for their viewpoints during the review, which was published as the Tickell Review in 2011 (Tickell, 2011). The coalition government in the UK has adopted many of Tickell's recommendations within the new EYFS.

Why was the EYFS introduced?

The EYFS was developed as a result of the growth in the amount of early years provision. The concern was not with the amount of provision but rather to ensure that all children received a good-quality start to their early life experiences and education. Research suggests that good-quality provision in all settings is important in that it will support the social and emotional development of children. Learning experiences with parents at home in collaboration with good-quality preschool provision have a positive impact on both the social and intellectual development of children. It has also been found that good-quality experiences before mandatory education are of particular benefit to **disadvantaged** children (Sylva et al, 2004). As stated above, the 2012 EYFS was introduced as a result of the findings of the Tickell Review of the 2008 EYFS. Main changes focus on minimising the bureaucracy involved with the 2008 EYFS. This was a concern for some of the practitioners working within early years. See the Pen Picture from a childminder later in this chapter for a practitioner's opinion of the EYFS.

At the end of reception, assessment will still take place against early learning goals but these have been reduced from 69 to 17 – three prime and four specific areas rather than the six curriculum areas within the 2008 EYFS will now be used. The three prime areas relate to:

- personal, social and emotional development;
- communication and language;
- physical development.

The four specific areas relate to:

- literacy;
- mathematics;
- expressive arts and design;
- understanding the world.

Children will still be assessed at the end of the EYFS but the focus will be more on goals needed for 'school readiness' in order to smooth the transition to Year 1. A development check will be carried on every two-year-old who is in a preschool setting in order to earlier identify children who are experiencing delay in development or who might have special educational needs. More emphasis will also be placed on working together effectively with parents (DfE, 2012b).

Pen picture – Sasha

It was my birthday and a colleague was leading circle time at the beginning of the preschool session. It was customary every morning for the children to say hello to each practitioner in turn and I was summoned to the carpet.

"1, 2, 3," she says and the children begin to sing *Happy birthday*. After they have finished, a four-year-old boy asks, "How old are you?" Naively I say, "I can't tell you that but it has a three and a five in it." "53," the boy replies. All of the staff burst into laughter. "I deserved that," I giggled.

Never underestimate a child's intelligence.

It is recognised in areas such as health that there is a correlation between birth weight, later long-term health and education achievement. Therefore input is needed from before birth and this recognition was given as motivation for the start of the Sure Start programme in England for the under-fours (see later in this chapter) and Head Start in the US for the under-sixes (Bertram and Pascal, 2002). (Head Start is a programme in America that was created in 1965. It is targeted on low-income families and provides the children with early years education, health, nutrition and parenting programmes.) The Minister for Sure Start, Catherine Ashton, said: 'We are at the beginning of a radical change in the way we deliver services for children and families to ensure all children get a sure start in life' (press release, March 2003, cited in Beckley et al, 2009, p 4).

It is clear that the aim of the EYFS is to provide a good-quality experience for children that compliments parental input in order to provide all children with the best start in life. It is a way to try to level the playing field (so to speak) for children in the UK in order to ensure that their start in life does not hold them back or disadvantage them.

A brief introduction to childminding

As mentioned above, childcare providers who works with children under the age of five must deliver the EYFS. This includes childminders and therefore all childminders in England must be registered with **Ofsted** and are inspected by Ofsted. In Wales, childminders are inspected by the Care and Social Services Inspectorate.

Ofsted

Ofsted is a government inspection body to ensure that all education provision is of a good quality, that the environment and premises are safe and that the activities and broader programme are stimulating. If the quality is not deemed to be suitable then it makes conditions and recommendations that must be addressed. The grading scale that inspectors follows is:

- grade 1: outstanding
- grade 2: good
- grade 3: requires improvement
- grade 4: inadequate.

Childminders provide childcare for one or more children under the age of eight. They work with children within their own homes or they work together (two or more childminders) in one of their homes, for payment. If you like to work for yourself, this is a good career opportunity as most childminders are self-employed and they set themselves up with their own childminding business. Different ratios exist depending on the age of the children that childminders care for. These ratios differ between England and Wales. The new EYFS provides for more flexibility within these ratios. The ratios include the childminder's own children and also other children in their care (foster children for example). Not all childminders will be registered for the maximum number of children. The maximum number of children they can care for will be determined during the home visits before registration. The premises will be inspected for suitability, space and safety before registration can take place. To become a childminder you will have to successfully complete a paediatric first aid course before you can register and you will have to successfully complete an Introductory Childcare course within six months of registering (NCMA, 2010).

Not all practitioners linked to the EYFS or Ofsted are always comfortable with the level of requirements and criteria that need to be met. However, as stated throughout this guide, the only constant is change and hopefully developments to a more positive and safe childhood for all children.

Pen picture – Dawn

In 1973 I trained in nursery work, the ethos was 'play with a purpose' – children played, adults joined in and we all had fun. We enjoyed each other's company and learnt as we went along.

After some years of working in day nurseries and bringing up our own family, I went into childminding. It was an easy step – I had the toys and the required safety equipment. I had to attend an introductory session and the house was checked out by the under 8s officer – I was given the go-ahead. It was lovely, the children were happy, they played and they learnt to make friends and be friends; life was fun.

Then we got Ofsted and the Early Years Foundation Stage and all that that entailed – inspections, risk assessments, written reports and policies. Time that would previously have been spent relaxing became paperwork time. Time that would have been spent playing with the children became time to check on their outcomes.

I don't think it made too much difference to the children: we made sure they still had fun, they went to school as well prepared as ever and they knew they were loved.

The Council for Awards in Care, Health and Education (CACHE) is a specialist awarding organisation that is a provider of relevant training. The CACHE level 3 Certificate in Childminding Practice is a useful qualification for existing childminders or for people thinking of pursuing a childminding career. The National Childminding Association was involved with the development of this course and therefore you can feel safe in the knowledge that it will provide you with the knowledge and skills you need. For more information about this and other childcare courses, please visit the following website: https://nationalcareersservice.direct.gov.uk and also: www.ncma.org.uk. If you are in Northern Ireland a useful website is: www.nicma.org/cms/index.php. If you are in Scotland a useful website is: www.childminding.org/

A brief introduction to Sure Start children's centres

Sure Start was established in 1998 as a result of the acknowledgement that deprivation is impacting on the lives of too many children and families in England. This grew into Sure Start children's centres with the aim of having a centre available for every community. Sure Start children's centres are a community resource for all families with children under the age of five.

It can be seen as a one-stop shop for service provision for families. It provides families with the opportunity to access all the services they might need to access in one place. Sure Start children's centres provide universal as well as targeted services. 'Universal services' refer to services that *all* children and young people need to access, for example healthcare and education. Targeted services, as the name suggests, refer to services that are targeted at particular children and young people. These can be provided within mainstream or universal settings and services. For example, a Sure Start children's centre provides universal services but also some individual services to children and parents who might need them. These additional needs may have been identified through the completion of an assessment, for example the Common Assessment Framework, which was introduced in the Children Act 2004. Specialist services refer to services that are offered to children and young people with very serious and complex needs, for example services for children with mental health issues and services for looked-after children. Sure Start children's centres provide a setting for a variety of these services to be delivered. Services offered include health and family support, which includes access to health visitors and midwifes and individual and group support for families with children with additional needs. Drop-in sessions and activities are offered with a wide variety of choice. These include mother and baby/toddler groups, young parents groups, parenting programmes, healthy eating projects and whatever other needs have been identified within the community. Information about local childcare and early education is provided as well as information and support with finding employment and/or relevant training. Some Sure Start children's centres also provides childcare for children under the age of five.

Pen picture – Lysette

I work in a nursery as a team leader and **inclusion** coordinator. I mainly work with the three- to five-year-olds but in my inclusion role I work with all ages. When I started the inclusion role it was called special educational needs co-ordinator; it changed after about three years. The change happened to make it friendlier for families being given support. It was felt that the special needs part was intimidating. My role changed as I felt it gave me the opportunity to include more children. I began to work with children who had additional needs that visited the Children's Centre with their parents and also with children who had speech impediments or delay. Hearing that I am an inclusion coordinator does not seem to concern parents as they may be being told their child needs extra support but not that they have a special need. My role is to plan for the children, support staff and communicate with parents to name a few responsibilities. I hope to continue my professional development in supporting children with additional needs.

In Sure Start children's centre's therefore, a wide range of roles is available to fit in with all of these activities and programmes on offer: Jobcentre Plus workers who assist parents in finding suitable training and employment, careers guidance workers, outreach workers, nursery workers (nursery teachers, nursery nurses and nursery assistants), health visitors, midwifes, social workers, qualified teachers, youth workers and so on. It is clear that Sure Start children's centres employ a number of different practitioners and professionals in a wide variety of roles and positions. A number of these professions are discussed across this chapter as well as Chapters Seven and Eight. For some of these roles, no post-compulsory education qualifications are needed to get started but for others professional qualifications at degree or postgraduate degree level are needed. In today's economic reality we would encourage you to volunteer or become involved in paid part-time or holiday work in order to build up some experience and a skills base to draw from. Experience will be crucial in interviews but also deciding what field you are ultimately interested in.

A brief introduction to preschools: playgroups and nursery schools

Preschools can be divided into two categories: playgroups and nursery schools. As we saw above, both playgroups and nursery schools in England must follow the 2012 EYFS.

Playgroups

Children can attend playgroups from two years nine months and some playgroups will even take children from the age of two years. Children can stay in playgroups until the age they start school. Playgroups are often run as registered charities and are non-profit-making. They are often run by groups of volunteers, which include parents. Playgroups are only open during term times and mostly offer half-day sessions for a number of days a week. Some playgroups are open for more hours per day. Half of the adults working at a playgroup must be qualified leaders or playgroup assistants.

Playgroups are run from a variety of settings. These can range from church and village halls, sports and community centres, scout huts to any other venue that can be hired by community groups. This does mean that the venue will not be used solely by the playgroup and therefore a lot of packing away of equipment and resources takes place at the end of each session. One of the positive points concerning this is that the venue is fully cleaned after each session and staff will be aware of broken toys and equipment. Children also learn that they are a part of a community that shares resources, including space.

So why would parents want their children to go to a playgroup? Playgroups are one of the service providers that tries to even out the playing field for young children in the UK. These settings provide children with preschool experiences that include arts and crafts, singing and dancing, outdoor and indoor play and initial learning experiences. They provide children with the opportunity to socialise outside the home environment, learn and develop, but they also aid with a **life stage transition**. They provide a safe 'stepping stone' between staying at home and starting school (Tameside Metropolitan Borough, 2011).

What training will you need if you want to work at a playgroup?

In both types of preschool settings (playgroups and nurseries) at least half of the staff must have suitable qualifications. You might be a parent thinking of volunteering at your child's setting to help out and to be a wider part of your child's education or you might want to get involved because you are interested in training or retraining as a playgroup worker. This is a good opportunity to get practical experience of working with this age range and also some relevant qualifications.

As a playgroup or preschool assistant you will need to undertake a relevant level 2 in Childcare Education. As a playgroup or preschool leader you will need to have successfully completed a level 3 course in Childcare Education or you must already be busy with it.

If you want to see a fuller list of more qualifications and information see:

■ www.bestbear.co.uk/childcare-information/preschool-playgroups.
php

- www.bestbear.co.uk/childcare-information/careers/childcare-qualifications.php
- https://www.pre-school.org.uk/practitioners/407/training

Nursery schools

Nursery schools (not the same as day nurseries) are more formal than playgroups in the way that they run their sessions. They are also often attached to a primary or a first school. Nursery schools provide a **vertical transition** between nursery, reception and compulsory education in a school setting. In some areas, playgroups are not available and therefore a nursery school is some children's first experience of group learning in a more formal environment. It provides children with a safe environment within which to become accustomed to being educated outside the home environment. As mentioned earlier in this chapter, this is also called a 'life stage' transition. Nursery schools normally consist of reception and nursery classes. A reception class will take children from the age of four. Nursery schools and nursery classes must have two adults in a room teaching between 20 and 26 children. One of these must be a qualified teacher and one a qualified nursery assistant.

A nursery teacher therefore needs to be a qualified teacher. Teacher training can be completed through an undergraduate degree and a postgraduate degree, work based or through what is known as School-Centred Initial Teacher Training. Before you can embark on any of these you will need to make sure that you have the necessary school-level qualifications. In England this is GCSEs (General Certificates of Secondary Education) in Maths and English and a science-based subject, with grades for each averaging between A and C. If you are from another country or education system then the equivalent will be accepted. You might also be able to take equivalency tests if you do not have these (they are tests to see whether you are able to achieve this standard of grades in these subjects). You will also have to pass some skills tests in numeracy, literacy and information and communication technology.

Pen picture – Alison

Every day I am blessed with happy, smiling faces, little people who are pleased to see and miss me when I'm not there, little people who call me 'Mum' by mistake and run up to me in the supermarket shouting my name so that everyone can hear them! Every day I am blessed with feedback that says I'm doing a good job – little people who steadily grow and become confident in their own abilities; every day there is something to marvel at. Of course there are the downsides – the paperwork, the constant need to prove myself on paper, forms for this, tick lists for that – but that's the adult stuff. I know when I'm doing a good job when little Tommy starts to read for himself, writes his own name independently and adds two digits without equipment and most importantly of all, Tommy wants to come to school and wants to learn. The satisfaction I get from being one of the people who has helped to inspire a child to love learning is, to use a common phrase, awesome. I love my job – that of being a teacher, sharing my skills and passions with others, a job which encourages me to be inventive and creative, a job which challenges me and a job which is never the same two days running – what more could anyone ask for from their career? If you are thinking about becoming a teacher, think long and hard – it's hard work, mentally, emotionally and physically, but the rewards are huge, life-affirming and endless!

Nursery assistant or nursery nurse

As a nursery assistant or nursery nurse you will be the second adult within a nursery school setting. You will help and support the nursery teacher with the tasks of the day. This includes being aware of health and safety and child protection, supporting children in their academic learning but also in their development of further skills, for example dressing and eating. You will help to plan and supervise arts and craft activities, music sessions, cooking activities and outings. You will appropriately share relevant information with the teacher as well as the parents.

So what qualifications do you need to become a nursery assistant/nursery nurse?

You can start by becoming a nursery assistant and work under supervision of someone else and then start an appropriate level 2 qualification. From September 2010 this could be the level 2 certificate in the Children and Young People's Workforce (Directgov, 2012a).

Pen picture – Emma

I have worked as a nursery nurse for the last eight years; my manager approached me and asked if I would consider studying for the foundation degree. At first I was very apprehensive as I am dyslexic and work full time; I also felt I would be unable to cope with the workload. The manager of the nursery stated that every setting required a member of staff to have this qualification. She said I would be the best person to do the foundation degree plus no one else was willing to go to university to study – this also added extra pressure. I spoke to my friends and family who gave me good advice and decided to do the foundation degree. I felt it would be an ideal time to study before I had other commitments like a family. Another plus was that my employers where going to fund the degree.

Since starting the foundation degree I feel it has made me a more confident person. I now find myself speaking out in situations I would normally keep quiet. I feel this is one of the reasons that I have recently been promoted.

After finishing the foundation degree I felt the need to carry on and gain the qualification BA Hons degree in Early Years. My employers decided against funding for this course; however, I felt that to further my career and gain enough knowledge to make me a good practitioner I should pay for it myself.

I have now started the BA Hons degree in Early Years. I have gained a great deal of knowledge, which I share with fellow members of staff. I have put a notice board in our staff room with different types of information that I have gathered from university to share and empower staff members with knowledge.

Even though it has been the hardest few years of my life I feel it has been worthwhile. I now have a foundation degree and I am studying for my full degree. Not only has it helped me with my promotion: I feel I now have greater opportunities, which will help to open many doors for my career. However, I feel the greatest achievement is the way in which it has made me grow as a person and boosted my confidence and self-esteem. When I finish the degree I plan to carry on studying and gain the early years professional status qualifications.

To become a nursery nurse you will have to complete a relevant level 3 qualification. From 2010 this is the Children and Young People's Workforce level 3 qualification but the following qualifications will also be accepted:

- CACHE level 3 Diploma in Childcare and Education;
- BTEC National Diploma in Children's Care, Learning and Development;
- NVQ level 3 in Children's Care, Learning and Development (Directgov, 2012a).

For some of the training courses, a work-based placement is needed. We, as the authors of this short guide, feel that this is a brilliant opportunity to link theory with practice and get some more relevant experience.

For more information about becoming a nursery nurse, go to the following website:

- https://nationalcareersservice.direct.gov.uk/advice/planning/ jobprofiles/Pages/nurserynurse.aspx

For more information about pre-schools go to:

- England: https://www.pre-school.org.uk/
- Wales: www.walesppa.org/
- Scotland: www.sppa.org.uk/
- Northern Ireland: www.early-years.org/

A brief introduction to being a nanny

Being a nanny can be a flexible arrangement for you but also for the family that you work for. Many parents do not hold nine-to-five jobs and therefore other provision might not meet their individual needs. Employing a nanny can also be a good option for families who have more than one child who needs looking after. As a nanny you will be employed by the parent. You do not have to be registered by Ofsted but you can register voluntarily on the Ofsted Childcare Register, which is a mandatory register for childcare providers for children from ages five to seven. It includes childminders and certain out-of-school providers.

A nanny is a childcare provider who works within the child's home environment. As a nanny you can be a live-in nanny or a nanny that only goes to the family home for certain hours on specified days. You might also be part of a nanny-share. This is where more than one family share a nanny so you will find yourself looking after children from more than one family.

Pen picture – Christine

Christine works as a nanny for two families. She considers herself lucky in that she used to look after the two small children of one family before they started school. When both the children entered school she was worried that her hours would be cut to after school only. This would have been difficult for her to do as she could not expect the family to keep her on for all the working hours in the day.

A friend of the family had to return to work after her maternity leave and the childminder who she was planning to send her baby to fell pregnant and therefore would be unable to look after her baby as well. Christine now looks after the baby in the morning; they have a different activity on every morning, such as music groups, baby and toddler groups, messy play and so on. After afternoon nap they go to fetch the other two from school and then they all have lovely afternoons together with the baby loving the attention from the older two but also loving watching them play!

Nannies have to successfully complete some relevant training in childcare and also need to be first-aid trained to work with children from birth upwards. This relevant training is the same as for a nursery assistant or nursery nurse but also included is the CACHE level 3 Diploma in Home-based Childcare (once again this was created with the National Childminding Association, so you know that it will provide you with the skills you need). Another positive point about this training is that it trains you to work in home-based settings with children from birth up to the age of 16. This will also therefore be a good qualification to gain if you are interested in au pairing. Since September 2010, the Children and Young People's Workforce certificate and diploma has replaced all the above qualifications but if you have already completed them you won't have to do the Workforce certificate (Directgov, 2012a).

For more information on becoming a nanny look at the following websites:

- https://nationalcareersservice.direct.gov.uk/advice/planning/jobprofiles/Pages/nanny.aspx
- www.ncma.org.uk (and click on all the links relating to being a nanny).

Issues that face children in early childhood

Children can face a variety of different issues during early childhood. They are at their most vulnerable and most dependent on their caregivers. The debate keeps on raging as to whether who children are and become is a result of nature or nurture or a combination of the two. Nurture links to the concept of the 'social construction' of childhood that we explored in Chapter Three. According to this idea, children are seen as 'separate', 'different' and 'dependent' on others in their earliest years. Chapter Four covering child development also familiarised you with the cognitive development theory, social learning theory and attachment theory relevant for the early years. According to the nurture viewpoint, humans are born as a blank slate and are impacted on and shaped by their environment and experiences. The nature viewpoint suggests that children are born with certain inherent qualities that will determine how they turn out in life. It is commonly accepted that people are a combination of nurture and nature in shaping who they become.

This illustrates some of the underpinning ideas that inform the government's attempts to 'level the playing field' for children's earliest experiences. Nurture and early education experiences can be impacted on by family and also by practitioners and professionals. Early care provision will enable children who might be disadvantaged in one or more areas to receive additional support or care. This disadvantage can be with regard to poverty, abuse or neglect of physical or emotional needs. Children of families who have moved from another country, perhaps where English is not spoken and the culture is very different, face particular issues with regard to language acquisition, learning cultural norms of behaviour and so on.

It is clear that the issues that children face during early childhood are linked to their immediate sphere of influence and significant relationships. According to Erikson (1968) (see Chapter Four), this starts with the immediate family and then extends to include school provision. It can therefore be seen as very beneficial for children during the early years to access further settings and service provision.

Other issues that children can face in early childhood relate to childhood illnesses and disease for which medical care and service provision will be needed. Unfortunately, this is outside the scope of this book, but if this is an area that interests you please bear in mind that all the roles discussed in this book will still be relevant. Chapter Nine will also provide you with a host of crucial information relating to difference. Playwork is discussed in the next chapter and can set you on the road to becoming a play specialist within a hospital setting (NHS, 2012).

The future of work with children during early years

As mentioned in Chapter Two, in May 2010 a coalition government consisting of the Conservative Party and the Liberal Democrat Party came to power in the UK. The biggest impact of this on the early years sector is the current ambiguous status of the Every Child Matters guidance. As mentioned previously, the original EYFS was introduced in September 2008 (before the General Election). A review of the EYFS was commissioned by the coalition government to ascertain the success and workability of the curriculum. Dame Claire Tickell published her report entitled *The early years: Foundations for life, health and learning* in 2011 and suggested some changes to the EYFS (Tickell, 2011). Overall, Dame Tickell (2011) made 46 recommendations. A number of these recommendations are now included in the new EYFS in England that came into force on 1 September 2012. We strongly recommend that you download and read the full review if you are interested in working within the early years sector.

SUMMARY OF KEY POINTS

In this chapter we have introduced you to:

- the idea of a curriculum that starts from birth – known as the Early Years Foundation Stage in England;
- the importance of the early years as a life stage;
- a number of professions who work with children during early childhood, including childminders, workers in children's centres, nursery nurses and assistants, nannies and au pairs;
- the issues that are faced by children during early childhood;
- the future of work with children during early childhood: introducing the Tickell Review.

FURTHER READING

A book that starts with the child development aspects that we covered in Chapter Four and links it with some of the practice settings and the EYFS that we covered in this chapter: Neaum, S. (2010) *Child development for Early Childhood Studies*, Exeter: Learning Matters.

A book that takes a large amount of the theory and ideas that we have explored in Part One of this book and links it directly to early childhood. It links with the social construction of childhood, child development and also some of the key skills that you need to be an effective practitioner in working with very young children: Parker-Rees, R., Leeson, C., Willan, J. and Savage, J. (eds) (2010*) Early childhood studies* (3rd edn), Exeter: Learning Matters.

A very accessible book introducing reflective practice within contemporary early years settings: Reed, M. and Canning, N. (eds) (2010) *Reflective practice in the early years*, London: Sage Publications.

ONLINE RESOURCES

To find out more about the roles that we discussed in this chapter as well as other roles within the sector, go to:

http://media.education.gov.uk/assets/Files/pdf/F/Foundations%20 for%20life%20health%20and%20learning.pdf

To find out more about the government's vision for families in the early years, go to:

www.education.gov.uk/childrenandyoungpeople/ earlylearningandchildcare/early

For a copy of the 2012 EYFS, go to:

http://media.education.gov.uk/assets/files/pdf/e/eyfs%20statutory%20 framework%20march%202012.pdf

7

working with children (aged six to 11)

In this chapter we will explore and examine the key theories and themes that underpin working with middle childhood specifically. We will also describe and consider some of the professions working with children from the age of six to 11 and explore the issues that are specific to this age group.

The importance of middle childhood

The age range from six to 11 years is known as middle childhood. In Chapter Three we introduced you to the concept of the 'social construction' of childhood and it was made clear that middle childhood is a life stage that did not always exist in history or in all cultures. Middle childhood starts from the age of six and, as we saw, this is the age when children in the past came to be seen as mini-adults and able to partake in the economic realities of life. Can you remember why this age? It occurred for a variety of reasons but the most noticeable ones were that children are able to communicate fluently at this age and are also not dependent on others to provide for their basic needs any more. Until the beginning of the 20th century, children in middle childhood were mostly seen in terms of their economic benefit (Fass and Mason, 2000). From the 20th century the dominant values in society changed for a variety of reasons (as explored in Chapter Three) and educating this age range became a priority. This led to the age range also being known as 'school age'.

As we saw in Chapter Four, during this age range, children become more socially involved with friends and peers, at school, before and after school and during weekend activities outside of the home and family environment. This is a time of great opportunities but also challenges for children as their social and educational worlds expand due to their cognitive as well as psychosocial development. During this age range, children have a lot of new skills and knowledge to gain. If they feel that they are not keeping up with their peers and friends it might lead to them feeling inferior and have an impact on their confidence (Erikson, 1968). Children in this stage of life experience transitions from primary to middle or secondary school and expansion of responsibilities. Physical growth starts to slow down during middle childhood and children develop their physical skills more, for example in sport. Children become prepubescent during this stage and some might be early maturers (reaching puberty earlier than their peers), which has a potentially different impact on the boys and girls in this age range.

Who works with children?

You might already be working with children in this age range or you might be considering the different options and opportunities available. We cannot help but reiterate what we wrote at this point in Chapter Six. It is important to remember that whatever age range you decide to work with, a knowledge and understanding of the whole of childhood is needed as it will inform your professional relationship and practice with the child and, where appropriate, their family.

The roles and activities that you might become involved in during this age range are diverse, fun and challenging. There will be overlap with some activities and roles within this age range, the early years and also in working with young people. This is why we were able to write one key skills chapter that stretches across all of Part Two of this book. A number of the practitioners described in this and other chapters in Part Two will work across different age ranges. For example, playworkers work with children from four to 16 years of age and nannies with babies right through to 16-year-olds. Other examples of people who work across different age ranges are teachers and social workers. A further example is the youth worker who runs a young parents group and will therefore work with young people but also babies, toddlers and children in middle childhood.

A variety of different roles and professions exist for working with children during middle childhood. This chapter aims to introduce you to some of them in order for you to have a more informed idea of the opportunities available to you.

Where you might work with children in middle childhood

Look back at Chapter Six at what we wrote about the three different sectors within public society in Britain. For each of the three age ranges that we distinguish in this book, practitioners can be found working across these three sectors.

Pause for thought and reflection

Think about and jot down all the middle childhood related jobs that you are aware of. Do you know in what sector these roles are found? Are they in the public, private or third sector?

Do you know anyone, either in a personal or professional capacity, who works with children in middle childhood? What is their job role? What type of work do they do? Who do they work for? If you are not sure of the answers to any of these questions, why not ask them whether you can talk to them about their jobs?

You do not have to do this exercise, but it might help you if you are thinking about a future career working with children in middle childhood. You will have already started your list of people to contact for advice or volunteering opportunities.

A brief introduction to au pairs

A number of young people think of au pairing as a gap-year opportunity. You can either be an au pair in your own country or more likely travel to another country and work there. Au pairs must be single with no dependants and be between the ages of 17 and 27. As an au pair you will stay with the family for a minimum of six months, look after children and fulfil other tasks that relate to the children, for example cooking, cleaning, taking them to activities and so on. In the UK, au pairs work in the family home for a maximum of five hours a day and of this time a maximum can be two evenings of babysitting, and they must have two full days off a week (therefore they work 25 hours a week). Au pairs have to receive a room of their own, meals as well as an allowance. Becoming an au pair is a great way to travel to other countries and to really immerse yourself in the culture of a different country. An au pair wanting to come to the UK normally does this to help them learn English and they can stay with a family for up to two years. You might consider au pairing in a country that you have an interest in or where you understand the language.

There is no specific required training and qualification to be an au pair (but bear in mind what we said about some of the nanny qualifications). This makes it a short-term option for someone who wants a gap year and is interested in working with children. You might try this as a working holiday opportunity or as a prospect to gain more experience of working with children. This will be a great opportunity for you to think about whether working with children is something you might want to pursue further. On your return to your home country you might decide to do more home-based childcare like becoming a nanny or working in another setting. A number of our students have had wonderful au pair experiences but others have found it more challenging. For example, as au pairs have no formal childcare qualifications or training they should not be looking after babies and children under school age without their parents being at home. Sadly, some au pairs do find themselves in this situation. If you experience anything that you are not happy or comfortable with, discuss it with the agency that you found the opportunity through. To find out more about working as an au pair, go to:

- www.direct.gov.uk/en/employment/understandingyourworkstatus/ workersemployeesandselfemployment/dg_198935
- www.bestbear.co.uk/childcare-information/au-pairs.php

A brief introduction to extended schools

In the UK the previous Labour government (1997–2010) pushed forward the extended schools agenda. According to this, children should have access to 'wraparound childcare', including before school in the mornings and also after school in the afternoons. This includes not only childcare but also activities that will bring together different services in order to address all areas of need of children, young people and their families. The underlying principle behind extended schools in the UK but also other countries such as North America is that mandatory education can only be effective 'once a range of welfare and health services were in place' (Smith, 2001). Extended schools therefore include specialist services for children and families to do with health, social care or special educational needs. They can also provide breakfast clubs, activity or sports clubs after school, homework clubs and other after-school clubs and provision. School facilities can be opened up to the rest of the community to enable space for mother and toddler groups and adult and lifelong learning sessions. This links back to the idea of the village college introduced by Henry Morris in Cambridgeshire, England in the 1920s. According to this system, schools are used for teaching children during the day and after school they become a learning environment for the whole community (Morris, 1925).

Within a school, some of the activities and clubs for children might be provided by teachers or non-teaching staff (Directgov, 2011c). The specialist services will be provided by specialist staff and professionals, for example social workers and health professionals. It is up to each school what extended services they provide, therefore not all of these services will be available at all schools.

If you want to be involved with extended schools you might consider being a teacher, teaching assistant or any other practitioner who works with children and young people – involved with either universal services or specialist services. Extended school provision might also make use of volunteers so contact your nearest school to find out whether and how you can get involved.

Pen picture – Nikki

Having worked within the banking industry for a number of years I decided that I wanted a new focus. Having three children of my own I began to realise the importance of a supportive network of childcare practitioners and a child's development and achievement. I also joined the school PTA [Parent Teacher Association], followed by becoming a school governor. Having no formal qualifications I had to start at the beginning with a level 2 childcare qualification. I then progressed to a level 3, then a foundation degree, BA Hons and finally a Masters in education. While studying I chose to work at the same time. I began by setting up my own mother and toddler group, followed by volunteering at a local preschool. On completing my level 2 I obtained paid work at a local lower school where I supported children who had emotional and social difficulties. I spent many hours playing board games, lying on toilet floors trying to persuade pupils to come back to lessons and chasing them around the playing field! On completion of my level 3 I also changed jobs and moved upwards to support pupils aged 9–13 in a local **middle school**. Again these children had issues with behaviour, self-esteem and emotional difficulties. This role was particularly rewarding as many pupils' lives were turned around with my help and other agencies' involvement. It was a pleasure to watch as these pupils made a successful transition to their upper schools (we have a three-tier education system) and go to achieve and have a positive outlook on life! I too have grown in confidence with my abilities and I share my experiences with my students who aim to carry on the good practice.

A brief introduction to playwork

Playwork in our opinion is undervalued as a profession. The main responsibility of playworkers is to plan and deliver appropriate play and leisure activities for children from the ages of four to 16. This is a vast age range so playworkers need to have a good knowledge base and understanding concerning the various types and stages of development of children and young people and also of the value of play across this age range.

Play is a way for children to reflect on their experiences and to make use of their experiences (Oliver and Pitt, 2011). Playwork provides children with the opportunities and resources they need to play. It is important for playwork practitioners to have knowledge and understanding of child development in order to identify the most appropriate activities to support children's development and crucially their enjoyment.

Playwork has its own set of professional principles. 'Playwork is a highly skilled profession that enriches and enhances children's play. It takes place where adults support children's play but it is not driven by prescribed education or care outcomes' (Skillsactive, 2011).

Playworkers work in a great variety of settings that span different timeframes but also different physical environments and settings. Playwork is delivered by the statutory, private and voluntary sectors. It can take place in both formal and informal settings and venues. The nature of the work can include breakfast clubs, lunch clubs, after-school clubs and care provision, mobile playbuses and also holiday schemes. Holiday provision can be open for a number of hours every day or consist of pop-up provision in local parks for a few hours here and there.

If you are interested in working with children across a broad age range and you like to have a very varied and active role then playwork might be for you! You could be involved in a variety of activities ranging from arts and crafts, sports and games, drama, singing and dancing, cooking activities, outings and many other leisure activities (Directgov, 2012b). Part of your remit would be to plan activities and leisure with children and young people's input.

Pause for thought and reflection

Why do you think it is necessary to involve the age range that you work with in your planning? Is this always possible? Can you think of ways that you can facilitate this involvement?

Pen picture – Leonie and Tracey

We organise activities for children aged three to 13 years old based on the EYFS, national curriculum, multicultural activities and national activities, but mostly our emphasis is on free choice and free play! We have varied backgrounds and have a wealth of childcare qualifications and experience. We are often undervalued and are often 'the poor cousins' as we offer affordable childcare. People think all we do is play [there's more to it behind the scenes]! Our main aims are to provide a happy safe stimulating environment for children to play, learn and have fun; we are here 100% for all our children. We care about the whole child and not just their academic levels and progression. We create an inviting space in which freely chosen play can take place, we observe and join in when invited. We teach children to risk assess, we encourage them to problem solve and learn new skills, including life skills. We plan areas for different play to take place in; the children choose what and where to play. We constantly update our learning and keep informed; to provide a valuable resource for our parents, and a reflective practice.

You do not need to have qualifications before you start working as a playworker. You can begin by volunteering first to gain experience then possibly move on to paid full-time or part-time work. Practitioners from a variety of backgrounds get involved in playwork, for example they may be a childminder, nanny, teaching assistant or nursery nurse. If you are, for example, a youth worker (see Chapter Eight) you might decide to get involved in playwork as there is an overlap in the age range that these two professions works with. Please remember that it is not necessary for you to come from a particular background; you might be a young person yourself wanting to volunteer in a playwork setting or to pursue a career in playwork. We all have to start our careers somewhere and your own life experience is a brilliant 'background' to start from!

While you are working or volunteering as a playworker you can complete a number of level 2 or level 3 playwork qualifications that are presented by a number of providers, for example CACHE or the BTEC. You can also qualify further with foundation degrees or higher national diplomas, or degrees that relate to playwork (Directgov, 2012b).

For more information on what it involves to be a playworker, go to:

- www.outofschoolalliance.co.uk/news.php
- https://nationalcareersservice.direct.gov.uk/advice/planning/jobprofiles/Pages/playworker.aspx

A brief introduction to social work

According to BASW, social work practice is focused on people. Social workers are professionals who work with vulnerable people from pre-birth to older people and aim to protect them from harm and enable them to live more independent lives.

Social workers are often employed in the public sector, by local authorities (that is, county councils or London boroughs), and can be found in departments known as adult or children's services. However, as a social worker you may also be employed by a range of voluntary or charitable organisations and in private settings. Wherever social workers are employed they work closely with the other professionals we will be examining in this chapter.

Pen picture – Lucy

Lucy had worked in a range of roles before deciding that the time was right for her to retrain as a social worker. She thoroughly enjoyed undertaking her placements in different settings when she was qualifying, not least of all as it gave her the opportunity to try working in ways and with different clients. She had worked with older people to identify support plans and enable them to live independently at home and she had also worked on a holiday scheme for young people, which was provided by a voluntary sector organisation. Both placements gave her the opportunity to learn new skills and how she spent her day was very different in each. It gave her the opportunity to decide that she would rather work with young people. Now she just had to decide whether she would prefer to work in child protection, children leaving care or within a voluntary sector role.

Since 2004 you need to gain a minimum of a degree in social work – BA (Hons) – in order to qualify as a social worker. You will need to provide evidence that you have had some relevant voluntary or paid experience in working in a similar field. You will also need to be able to illustrate that you have done your homework, know what the social work professional values and code of practice are and have a political awareness of government agendas and policy changes on relevant subjects.

When applying to a university to study, depending on where it is, you should check that the course is approved or accredited by:

- the General Social Care Council (www.gscc.org.uk/) (England);
- the Care Council for Wales (www.ccwales.org.uk/);
- the Northern Ireland Social Care Council (www.niscc.info/); or
- the Scottish Social Services Council (www.sssc.uk.com/).

These are also the bodies that you will also have to register with upon graduation. As social workers work with many of the most vulnerable people in society, they have to maintain their registration if they wish to continue to practise as social workers. This is so that the people who use the services provided by social workers, services users as they are called, can be sure that professionals can be trusted.

A brief introduction to parent support advisers

Parent support advisers provide advice and support to parents and families with regard to parenting, attendance issues but also any further (health, social care and educational) issues that might need intervention (early or late) within the family.

Even though we are specifically introducing parent support advisers here we are also referring to other roles where support is offered to parents. The job titles and also job roles for parent practitioners vary significantly from local authority to local authority, within the voluntary and community sector and also the private sector.

Pause for thought and reflection

Think of the job that you are interested in doing in future or that you might already have experience in. This does not have to be with middle childhood but can be with the early years or young people. Can you identify ways that you might need to support parents in this role? Depending on the role that you are thinking about, this might be a job where parent support is a key part of your role, an important part but not the main role or a job where it might happen but it is on the periphery.

The role of parent support adviser was introduced by the last Labour government's chancellor in a report entitled *Support for parents: The best start for children* (HM Treasury and DfES, 2005). It was part of New Labour's strategy to level the playing field for all children and young people (**equal opportunities**). The first interim report of the pilot suggested that the role of parent support adviser has three key principles: 'rights and responsibilities: supporting parents to meet their responsibilities to their children; progressive universalism: support for all, with more support for those who need it most; and prevention: working to prevent poor outcomes for children, young people and their parents from developing in the first place' (Lindsay et al, 2007, p 1).

To work as a parent support adviser you will need to undertake some training and gain qualifications. Parent support advisers can start to work within this role without relevant qualifications but will mostly have some experience in working with children, young people and crucially their families. Parent support advisers will normally gain level 2 or level 3 qualifications in related courses. These can be in, for example, social care or childcare. They can also be qualified teachers or counsellors or be a holder of a relevant undergraduate or postgraduate degree (Little, 2010).

The parenting practitioner workforce involves a number of roles across the different sectors. Therefore it is almost impossible to identify one specific qualification or training that is needed. A number of parenting practitioner roles are highly specialised, for example social workers, midwives, educational psychologists and teachers. These roles require a level 6 qualification that is equivalent to a BA (Hons) degree at university. Other roles are less specialised and can include, for example, housing support (Little, 2010).

Parent support advisers and education welfare officers (whose role we will introduce you to in Chapter Eight) work closely together in order to ensure the best service provision for a family. When we were in practice we would refer to the relationship between a parent support adviser and an education welfare officer as that of 'good cop, bad cop'. The parent support adviser is the 'good cop' who aims to support and encourage positive parenting. The education welfare officer, on the other hand, is the one who has to 'lay down the law' so to speak and discuss the consequences for both children and parents of, for example, non-attendance at school. This is a good example of a situation where multi-agency working and information sharing are key to finding a successful outcome for the whole family involved. Other practitioners might also become involved in the situation, for example a youth worker who can do some work with the young person who is not attending school regularly. In working with children and young people, any practitioner who thinks that their input and role are the most important or life-changing for their clients needs to go back to the basic skills and also reflect on their personal values and the professional ethics that they have to adhere to. As individuals, teams and organisations working together we are able to provide children, young people and their families with the most positive and valuable input for their individual realities.

Pen picture – Lisa

The parent support worker (PSA) role was implemented over five years ago and was designed to work within a cluster of primary/secondary schools delivering child-centred as well as a parent-focused approaches. Their main remit was to build positive relationships between schools and parents in order to improve attendance, behaviour and support children's development as well as learning.

As the role has evolved, PSAs have become an integral part of the localities, evidenced in their ongoing support through direct work, liaison with families at home, signposting to other services and parenting programmes.

Issues faced by children during middle childhood

As with the other chapters that focus on working with specific age ranges, children during middle childhood also have particular issues that are key to their developmental stage and transition period. A key concern from the age of five is the start of mandatory education in England, Wales and Scotland and four in Northern Ireland. As was seen in Chapter Three on the social construction of childhood, this mandatory education starting age varies across countries. The social construction of childhood reflects not just an individual country's thinking concerning children and education but also its economic, political and social environment.

During middle childhood, children experience the transition from primary to secondary school or in a three-tier system the transition from first school to middle school. This vertical transition is a key issue during this life stage and a number of professions provide support and advice to help children and parents cope with it. Mechanisms that help people to cope with difficult or new situations are also called resilience factors (Newman and Blackburn, 2002). According to Newman and Blackburn (2002, p 1), '[r]esilient children are better equipped to resist stress and adversity, cope with change and uncertainty, and to recover faster and more completely from traumatic events and episodes'. Practitioners working with children, young people and their families are resilience factors for their clients experiencing a transition or other difficult situations.

Family time is lacking in the UK. This is in sharp contrast to some other countries, for example Spain and Sweden, where time for spending with children is more readily available. Long working hours in demanding, pressurised jobs can be blamed for this. In Spain and Sweden, time spent with extended family is also more readily available. In the UK families tend to look more towards the state and also private provision to cater for their children outside of school hours. 'My sister picks them up after school and takes them to her house for lunch, I prefer that they spend time with family, rather than more time at school', Spanish ethnography, mother (Ipsos MORI and Naim, 2011, p 31).

Pause for thought and reflection

What are your thoughts on this? Do you think the government should be responsible for children before and after school and during holidays or should parents be making their own arrangements for their children?

A main concern during this age range is the difficulty in finding a balance between health and safety and still allowing children to explore their environments and for them to take risks. Risk taking in play is key but sadly our health and safety culture is limiting risk-taking behaviour for children. As a result of fear of danger but also fear of being sued, children's play areas and school playgrounds have been made 'overly' safe. This is, however, not a new state of affairs. In 1995, the-then head of playground safety at the Royal Society for the Prevention of Accidents said: 'We have made playgrounds so monumentally boring that any self respecting child will go somewhere else to play, somewhere more interesting and usually more dangerous. The play value in them is so limited that it barely scores on any register of play value' (Heseltine, 1995, p 92, cited in Ball, 2007, p 72).

Children as consumers is an issue that has received a lot of attention in research studies, government reports and the media. However, in a recent report (Ipsos MORI and Naim, 2011, p 4) it was found that: 'Behind the statistics we find many UK children do not refer to material goods when talking about what makes them happy, and also understand the principles of moderation in consumption, but may have parents who feel compelled to purchase, often against their better judgement.'

Consumerism is a key concern; however it is indicative of a broader issue within our society. This children's wellbeing study (Ipsos MORI and Naim, 2011, p 70) found that:

> Children want time with their parents, good relationships with their friends and lots of stimulating things to do. In the UK we find parents struggling to find time to be with their children or to help them participate in sporting

and creative activities but instead feeling compelled to purchase consumer goods which are often neither wanted nor treasured. Consumer goods play a multi-faceted role in children's lives – sometimes positive and sometimes negative – and there is no doubt that status technology and clothing brands play their part in creating or reinforcing social divisions between the 'haves' and the 'have-nots'.

An issue that is a concern for the practitioners in the field rather than the children is the uncertainty and constant changes within the social policy arena. As we indicated in Chapter Two, the only constant to be expected in this regard from a practitioner's perspective is change.

The future of work with children

The New Labour government (1997–2010) had a clear strategy for children and young people's services as communicated and directed through the Every Child Matters agenda. The Conservative and Liberal Democrat coalition is not yet entirely clear about its strategy. It is clear, however, about the fact that it thinks that New Labour's promises are unaffordable. This section will introduce readers to the coalition's vision for the future of children's services.

The coalition government's focus is on specialised rather than universal services. Due to a shortage of money and a **budget deficit**, the government has decided that it is necessary to make cuts in service provision. This has had a significant impact on children and young people's services. One of the services that we introduced in this chapter – playwork – has been severely hit by these cuts. Play England had the following to say about the cuts:

> Our work with local communities to support them in providing for their own children's play is exactly what the Big Society is supposed to be all about but it will be difficult to continue without government support. We are calling on each of the governing parties to think again; to be true to their rhetoric about play, and to make it the priority that it is for children and families. Play England's work will continue in spite of the

reduced circumstances that we will now face, and announcements about our new structure and work programme will be made as soon as these are finalised. (Play England, 2011)

Playwork is not the only service that has been affected by the cuts. In the next chapter we introduce another profession that has been severely affected – youth work.

The government is not proposing that as a result of funding cuts no services should be delivered. No, instead the aim is for local communities to become involved and to deliver services themselves. The Big Society is the brain-child of David Cameron and is built on the ideals of community spirit, voluntary engagement and communities doing it for themselves. With regard to the future we have already had a taste of the implications of the Big Society and funding cuts with regards to reduced service provision. How the Big Society and volunteering will impact on quality and sustainability of service provision still remains to be seen.

SUMMARY OF KEY POINTS

In this chapter we covered working with middle childhood. The chapter introduced you to the following:

- the importance of middle childhood;
- an exploration of who works with children in this life stage;
- what extended schools are and what roles are available within them;
- the importance of play for children and the playwork profession;
- the variety of parent practitioner roles with a specific focus on parent support advisers;
- issues that children face during middle childhood;
- the Big Society and volunteering as service provision for children and their families.

FURTHER READING

An interesting read on how the UK's children compare to other children with regard to wellbeing: UNICEF (2007) 'Innocenti Report Card 7', *Child poverty in perspective: An overview of child well-being in rich countries: A comprehensive assessment of the lives and well-being of children and adolescents in the economically advanced nations*, Florence: UNICEF Innocenti Research Centre, www.unicef-irc.org/publications/pdf/rc7_eng.pdf

The book for you if you are at all interested in playwork. It looks at the role of staff in providing play opportunities for children and young people and identifies and discusses playwork provision in England, Scotland, Wales and Northern Ireland. It also critically looks at the future of playwork, as well as qualifications and training that are available: Brown, F. and Taylor, C. (eds) (2008) *Foundations of playwork*, Maidenhead: McGraw-Hill/Open University Press.

A wonderful book for additional reading about the importance of parenting but also parenting support. Remember that whatever age range during childhood that you will work with, parents and carers are part and parcel of a child's life and therefore your role. Easy, accessible reading that also introduces the policy context: Miller, S. (2010) *Supporting parents*, Maidenhead: McGraw-Hill/Open University Press.

ONLINE SOURCES

To read all the playwork principles in full, go to: www.skillsactive.com/our-sectors/playwork/early-years-foundation-stage/item/3298/3298

To find out more about the support services that are available for families at risk study the following pdf document: Department for Children, Schools and Families' *Think family toolkit*, www.yor-ok.org.uk/Catalyst/Think%20Family%20Toolkit.pdf

To view relevant videos to do with professions working within the early years, middle childhood and young people, go to: www.teachfind.com/teachers-tv/working-parents-common-issues-secondary-parent-support-advisors-psas (there is a very interesting interview with a parent support adviser).

8

working with young people (aged 11 to 19)

Introduction

As we have seen in previous chapters, there are many different professionals who work with children and young people from a range of different perspectives. In this chapter we will explore and examine the key theories and themes that underpin working with young people specifically. We will also describe and consider the various approaches to working with young people aged 11 to 19 and explore the issues that are specific to this age group.

The importance of adolescence and youth

As we saw in Chapter Four, adolescence can be seen as a distinct life stage whereas the term 'youth' refers to a wider age range. Professionals and organisations who work with young people often consider their target group as ranging from 11 to 19 years old.

However, they can work with young people aged up to 25 if they have particular needs such as a learning difficulty. Given the global recession and the impact this has had on young people aged 19 to 25, we may see more professionals targeting their work to support these older young adults, particularly regarding issues of education, employment and housing. Unfortunately, we do not have the remit to address these issues within this book, but you might want to research and consider these factors further.

Adolescence is a holistic life stage that incorporates all aspects of a young person's life. It is a period that is characterised by transitions, their peers, their families and the cultural context in which they live. As we have begun to explore in Chapters Three and Four of this book, it is also a period of great change in terms of young people's physical, social, emotional and cognitive development. Yet during these turbulent times, where young people are fluctuating between childhood and adulthood, in the UK we expect them to be mature enough to make choices that will potentially affect their entire adult life. An example of this is the choices they make of which subjects to study at GCSE or standard grades and A Levels or Advanced Highers, which will potentially impact significantly on their future careers.

Many practitioners who work with young people do so in or through the young people's school environment. Schools are also known as **formal education**, as the classes are planned around a formal environment (a classroom) and a formal curriculum (the topics studied). Working with young people within their school can support them within this environment and enable them to achieve more than they would otherwise. For the most part, working with young people through their school is important because that's where the young people are and there are also the structures in place to support their engagement and participation and maintain their well-being.

However, it is also important to work with young people outside the formal education system. Primarily this is because not all young people attend school regularly if at all. The young person may be home-schooled or excluded from school either permanently or temporarily. They may be a **school refuser** or not attend for religious or cultural beliefs.

It is also important to remember that young people only formally attend school between the hours of 9am and 3pm, during school weeks. This means that they potentially need somewhere to go before and after school, at weekends and during the holidays. As society has changed and government policy has developed there has been a shift in parental working patterns. The Labour government introduced an initiative to support mothers to go back to work as part of its strategy for reducing child poverty (Northall and Smith, nd). For many working people their day may start at 9am and finish at 5pm, but commuting may add at least an hour either side of those times. Therefore children and young people may need somewhere to be before school and for up to three hours after school.

As we saw in Chapter Seven, this initiative was supported by the development of extended schools (Directgov, 2011c), which saw a range of organisations supporting and working with schools to provide wraparound provision. It was also complemented by Sure Start children's centres and other initiatives we discussed in Chapter Six.

Who works with young people?

You may already be interested in a career working with young people or just interested to know about the range of professionals who might be working with them. You will find professionals working with this age group where ever the young people are at. This can be where the young people are at geographically, that is, in schools (teachers, learning support assistants and youth workers) or on street corners (outreach or detached youth workers). Alternatively, it can be where they are at personally, perhaps emotionally or developmentally (educational psychologists), supporting them to address family issues (social workers), develop social skills (youth workers) or find work (Connexions/Careers Guidance).

Where you might work with young people

Look back at Chapter Six at what we wrote about the three different sectors within the public society in Britain. For each of the three age ranges that we distinguish in this book, practitioners can be found working across these three sectors.

Pause for thought and reflection

In your daily life or through previous experiences, jot down every youth-related organisation you can think of or have had an experience of. Do you know whether they are in the public, private or third sector?

Do you know anyone, in either a personal or professional capacity, who works with young people? What is their job role? What type of work do they do? Who do they work for? If you are not sure of the answers to any of these questions, why not ask to talk to them about their work?

You do not have to do this exercise, but it might help you if you are thinking about a future career working with young people. You will have already started your list of people to contact to discuss volunteering with or for advice.

There are a number of differing roles for practitioners within the different sectors, as we have previously stated. Many of practitioners are predominantly found working within the public or voluntary and community sectors. These include youth workers, Connexions personal advisers, social workers, education welfare officers and Youth Offending Team (YOT) members. As we identified in Chapter Four, there have been a number of policy changes that have affected those working with children and young people since 1997. With each different policy change and refocus, practitioners have often found their work realigned to fit new government policy. Often this has seen a change in their job title, for example from youth worker to youth support worker. However, throughout these changes their professional values and perspectives, often underpinned by distinct professional qualifications, have remained the same. So too have the reasons why they want to go into these professions, that is, to make an impact on the lives and development of future generations, to make a difference to society or because they consider their work a **vocation**.

The role of volunteering

In this chapter we are going to take a very brief look at some of the main professions working with young people. However, we should also acknowledge the important roles provided by volunteers. Many of the professional colleagues who we know started their careers by volunteering, including ourselves. In fact it is one of the best ways to get into working with young people. So while we are introducing you to different professional roles, we recognise that many people 'working' with young people are actually doing so voluntarily.

For some people, volunteering for two and a half hours a week in a youth club or being a volunteer panel member for a YOT meets their needs. They may enjoy their work, but like so many others, they may be looking for a way to 'give back' to their local community, 'make a difference' or just to get out and meet new people. Others will be volunteering as a step up in their profession and to gain needed experience. All the services that work with young people vitally need a broad range of volunteers to ensure that they run smoothly and effectively; in fact many projects and services would shut completely without the support of volunteers. While we use the term 'professional' in this book to refer to people who are professionally qualified, the authors would like to explain that this does not mean we think that volunteers are 'amateur' practitioners. In fact, most volunteers have an array of transferrable skills that they bring from their 'day jobs' and the life skills they have learnt.

A brief introduction to Careers Guidance/Connexions

Before Connexions was developed in 2000 as a result of the Learning and Skills Act 2000, young people were supported by a more generic Careers Guidance service. However, unlike its predecessor, Connexions offers independent advice and guidance to young people on a range of issues such as education, housing and finance as well as 'careers' in its strictest sense. Until 2008, a number of Connexions Partnerships delivered the work at a local level. However, on 1 April

2008, the duty to provide the Connexions service was transferred to local authorities. While Connexions nationally has a very strong brand identity, young people's and partners' experience of the service has tended to be different in local areas.

We identify at various points in this book that there is a great need to support young people with issues regarding their employment. Unfortunately, since the coalition government came to power in 2010 there have been a number of changes to the Connexions service amidst a period of austerity and massive changes nationally. While, there is an argument that careers guidance will be needed for young people in both good times and bad, in June 2012 youth unemployment hit 1.1 million (Rhodes, 2012). Even if this issue can be addressed quickly, there will be implications for this generation of young unemployed people for years to come. The coalition government's all-age National Careers Service launched in April 2012 (BIS, 2012). There is no longer an expectation that Connexions will be delivered by local authorities, therefore it will be a local decision as to what happens to the service. We therefore suggest that if you are interested in supporting young people with their career choice, you start by contacting your local council to see what decisions have been made locally.

Pen picture – Nick

Nick was a Connexions intensive personal adviser. He spent a lot of time working one-to-one with young people at risk of not being in education, employment or training (NEET). He worked closely with his local youth work team as they often referred young people to him who needed his extra intervention and allowed him to use their facilities when working with young people.

There were a number of changes in the structure of his team and he was redeployed as a young people's worker. A lot of his job is quite similar to his old role as the youth work team is now doing more targeted work. However, he now works with groups too. He likes his job and has enjoyed the challenges and training, but he is also keeping an eye on developments in the National Careers Service just in case he wants to apply for a job in the new programme.

While there have been a lot of changes in his role in the last few years, he is pleased that his experience and qualifications have provided him with a great many opportunities.

Given that each local authority will decide on the role and nature of Connexions in its area in the future, we cannot state categorically what qualifications might be needed in areas where Connexions will still exist. However, to become a careers adviser in the new National Careers Service you can study via higher education (at university) or through work-based qualifications with a level 3 Award for Supporting Clients to Overcome Barriers to Learning and Work, a level 4 Diploma in Career Information and Advice or a level 6 Diploma in Career Guidance and Development (NCS, 2012).

For more information, take a look at the following websites:

- the Institute of Careers Guidance (www.icg-uk.org/);
- the National Careers Service (https://nationalcareersservice.direct. gov.uk/advice/planning/jobprofiles/Pages/careersadviser.aspx).

A brief introduction to education welfare

Education welfare officers (EWOs) work with school-aged children and young people, their families and schools to tackle poor attendance at school. In most nations of the UK, you will find that EWOs form part of an education welfare service working for the local authority. They have a role in informing parents of their legal responsibility to ensure that their child goes to school; supporting families to access the full range of benefits available to them, such as free school meals; as well as taking action through the magistrates' courts if children and young people continually fail to attend school.

Pen picture – Sara

Ex-teacher Sara has been working as an EWO for a range of reasons, not least of all as it fits in well with the fact that she has a young son, as she works term-time only. EWOs used to work as an independent service but are now part of the local authority multidisciplinary teams. As an EWO, Sara has responsibility for two secondary schools and their feeder primaries. She regularly meets with senior leadership representatives in the secondary school on a weekly or fortnightly basis and primaries on a monthly, half-termly or termly basis. During this time she will identify pupils with an attendance of 85% or less. There are valid reasons why pupils maybe absent and Sara is able to advise schools on reducing this but mainly she works with pupils who have unauthorised absence or are seen to be truanting. Once the pupils have been identified and the school has done what it can to improve the attendance, Sara will visit the family and pupil to try to make them aware of the legal consequences of non-attendance and establish what the reason behind the absence is. It is at this time that Sara will be able to signpost the family to other support in the form of parent support advisers and young people's workers or to set up meetings with the school if there are issues that need addressing there. If the attendance does not improve in a given time then Sara will be able to issue fixed penalty notices to the parents, or proceed to prosecution in the magistrates' court.

The role of the EWO is a varied one, which requires a range of skills and knowledge. There are no specific qualifications for working within education welfare, but most employers will expect you to have a qualification in a relevant field such as social work, teaching or youth work.

For more information, take a look at the following websites:

- the National Careers Service (https://nationalcareersservice.direct. gov.uk/advice/planning/jobprofiles/Pages/educationwelfareofficer. aspx);
- the Skills4Schools (www.skills4schools.org.uk/page.asp?id=316).

Alternatively, contact your local school or academy and see if there is an EWO who would be willing to talk to you about their work.

A brief introduction to educational psychology

Educational psychologists work with children and young people to tackle issues that they are having with their education. They do this in a range of different ways, for example working face to face with individuals or groups of children and young people. Their role involves the assessment of children and young people's learning and emotional needs and identifying ways to meet these needs. Alternatively, they may be involved in undertaking research and informing policy decisions at a strategic level.

Pen picture – Charlie

Charlie always wanted to be an educational psychologist. This is important as it is a very specialist role that has taken Charlie a long time to qualify in. His role sees him working with children and young people to assess whether they need any extra or specialist support to help them to develop. Just like Sara, the EWO, educational psychologists are usually in a 'link' role, which means that they are responsible for a number of schools and their time is shared between them. Charlie is in his final year of training, which means that he spends a number of days working with a local authority and the rest of the week studying at college. It is hard work at times, and challenging, but Charlie has found it hugely rewarding. There is a lot of diversity in his role as he may visit different schools to assess a child or young person. He also works with the professionals who support the children and young people on a daily basis to identify ways for the children and young people to progress.

Psychologists study psychology in general before specialising in a certain area such as education, health or occupational psychology. This is usually through a university degree, which should be accredited by the British Psychological Society and would enable you to have Graduate Basis for Chartered Membership (Directgov, 2011d). To become an educational psychologist you will need a Doctorate in Educational Psychology. You should ensure that any course you want to study is approved by the Health & Care Professions Council.

For more information, take a look at the following websites:

■ the Health and Care Professions Council (www.hpc-uk.org/education/programmes/register/);
■ the British Psychological Society (www.bps.org.uk/).

If you are interested in working in this field, it will take a lot of hard work and commitment to qualify so once again we strongly urge you to talk to someone who is already working in this area to ensure that it is the job for you!

A brief introduction to teaching

You may already have a good idea of what you think being a teacher is all about from your own experience. You may be right, but there may be more to the profession than meets the eye. Teachers don't just work in the traditional classroom: they can also be found working with children and young people in alternative education settings as well as with those children and young people who are taught at home while ill or due to exclusions.

It is also important to note that the role of a teacher is very varied, with pastoral duties that might involve being a tutor or head of year or being involved in the Duke of Edinburgh scheme or other school-based clubs.

Of course there are also various types of teaching, that is, primary, secondary and further or higher education. You can also opt to go in to specialist areas such as teaching young people with special educational needs. For comprehensive guidance on the different types of teaching at each age, take a look at the National Careers Service website (https://nationalcareersservice.direct.gov.uk/advice/planning/jobprofiles/).

Pen picture – John

John was working in sales after graduating with a degree in geography. After some time reflecting on his future career options he decided to retrain as a secondary school teacher. He remembered his school days well, so thought he knew what to expect. While not expecting to feel quite so old and having to get used to being called 'sir', he was most surprised by the range of extra-curricular activities that went on at the academy school he trained in. He soon realised that as well as his love of geography he had the opportunity to indulge in his love of the outdoors by getting involved in the Duke of Edinburgh project at his school. He thoroughly enjoyed working alongside youth workers from the local authority and voluntary sector and sharing his skills with young people half way up a mountain – something he would never have visualised when he first thought of entering teaching.

There are a number of different routes through which you can gain your qualified teacher status (QTS). All these routes involve you successfully completing a period of initial teacher training (ITT). These include undergraduate, postgraduate, school-centred initial teacher training (SCITT) and work-based (NCS, 2012). One of the most popular routes from employers' perspectives, the Graduate Training Programme, has been replaced by the School Direct Training Programme.

For all four of these routes you will need at least an undergraduate (degree) level qualification, usually in the area that you wish to teach, by the time you achieve your QTS. With this range of options you can either identify that you want to go into teaching in the future and choose a suitable degree programme or gain QTS via a Post Graduate Certificate in Education (PGCE) in order to teach young people in the subject area of your degree. This means that wherever you are in your career, teaching could be an option for you.

If you think that teaching might be something that you are interested in, take a look at the Get into teaching (http://www.education.gov.uk/get-into-teaching/teacher-training-options.aspx) or the Training and Development Agency for Schools (TDA) (www.tda.giv.uk) websites. If you know any teachers it would also be beneficial to talk through their experiences with them.

Teaching may not be a route that is appropriate for you, but you might still be interested in working with young people in a school setting. You can work with young people in a range of different capacities in a school in 'allied' professions, for example as a learning support assistant or teaching assistant. Again, we suggest that you take a look at the National Careers Service website (https://nationalcareersservice.direct.gov.uk/) and speak to professionals working in that area.

A brief introduction to youth offending

Youth offending teams (YOTs) were established in England and Wales in 1988 through the Crime and Disorder Act 1998. These teams are overseen by the **Youth Justice Board** at a national level but they are managed by local authorities. They are multidisciplinary teams, as we discussed in Chapter Four, so professionals can be seconded to them from other teams or employed from a range of different perspectives such as youth work, social work and so on.

Professionals working within these teams work with young offenders, both individually and in groups, aiming to prevent offending and reoffending. YOTs work with young people at all stages of the justice system so may find themselves working in secure institutions, courts and community reparation projects.

In Scotland, the work of the 32 local authorities is overseen by the National Youth Justice Advisory Group (Scottish Government, 2011) and in Northern Ireland it is overseen by the Youth Justice Agency.

Pen picture – Raj

Raj has been working with young offenders for a number of years. Originally he had started his career working with young people as a youth worker. Through the process of becoming professionally qualified he was expected to do a number of placements, one of which was within a YOT. This experience helped him to realise that this was the area of work for him and he hasn't looked back.

It is a challenging job, but this is something Raj relishes, that and the fact that no two days are the same. As he is working with very high-risk and vulnerable young people he finds his youth work experience invaluable. The sorts of things he might do in his job include supporting young people who have offended to identify action plans to prevent them from reoffending; supporting young people who have offended to get back into education or work; and supervising young offenders after their release from secure institutions if they are on court orders and community sentences. All the things he does in his job have to be properly recorded and so Raj has to evaluate his work, keep up-to-date case notes, carry out risk assessments and write reports for the courts.

One of Raj's favourite aspects of his work, apart from working with the young people, is the range of other practitioners he works with. Through his career so far, Raj has had to support young people in almost every aspect of their life in order to support them to adjust to life after release from a secure institution and hopefully to not reoffend. So he could be in contact with housing officers, social workers and substance misuse workers to meet the young people's welfare needs or educational institutions or potential employers.

Most professionals working in a YOT have a relevant professional qualification in an area such as probation, social work or youth work. Therefore you are likely to need a degree-level qualification; however, in some areas it is possible to start as a YOT support worker. While this does not require such a high-level qualification, you would still be expected to have a lot of experience working with young people.

This is a very brief introduction to a very broad field of work. There are various practitioners who may work within this area such as probation officers, substance misuse workers and victim care officers. If you think that you might be interested in this field more broadly, you should do your research. The National Careers Service website is a great resource and would be a good place to start as it will signpost you to further resources (https://nationalcareersservice.direct.gov. uk/). For more information about the role and remit of members of a YOT, take a look at the Youth Justice Board website (www.justice. gov.uk/about/yjb/).

A brief introduction to youth work

Professionals who consider themselves youth workers can have a number of different job titles, for example youth support workers, youth development workers or youth and community workers. They work wherever young people are 'at', that is, geographically or socially and emotionally. This means that it is a very diverse profession and so it is difficult to condense this into a few paragraphs. You may work in a hospital, for a social housing landlord or for the army welfare service with a youth work qualification. You might find yourself abseiling off a bridge as a summer camp counsellor in the US, leading a group of young people with a range of physical and learning disabilities on a Duke of Edinburgh expedition or working one-to-one with a young person at risk of exclusion from school. You might well also find yourself working in a 'traditional' youth club on a Friday night; such is the diversity of the work. As Smith (2002) states:

> The meaning of the term 'youth work' is difficult to pin down. When people talk about youth work they can mean very different things. For example, they might be describing work with a group of Guides; running a youth club; making contact with different groups of young people on an estate; mentoring a young person; or facilitating a church fellowship; or tutoring on a mountain walking course.

Wherever youth workers work with young people they adhere to key principles that have been defined by Smith (2002) as being focused on young people and underpinned by their **voluntary engagement** with youth work services. Youth workers are committed to **association** as well as creating an informal, friendly but professional environment. Finally youth workers aim to create the right environment for young people to learn about themselves, others and the world around them, hopefully developing themselves and promoting their welfare and well-being.

Pen picture – John

John is a professionally qualified youth support worker. He is aware that there appear to have been a lot of changes in his professional sphere over the last few years; however, he does not feel that this has materially affected his relationships and working practices with young people. As a professional member of the team, his training has supported him to work in a certain way with young people, whether it is a targeted group set up to work with young fathers or within the youth club he runs, which is funded by a parish council. In the recent restructures he had the opportunity to apply for a more managerial post. While he wouldn't mind doing that at some point in the future, at the moment he doesn't want to do anything that takes him completely away from working face to face with young people, whether that be individually or in groups. He also enjoys the varied nature of his job. He likes working with young people on a Friday night to ensure that they have something positive to engage in where alternatively they might drink due to boredom. He also enjoys his detached project where he works with young people on the streets of a local housing estate. The group that has developed through this project is working together to plan a residential in the summer and John wouldn't miss out on being there to celebrate their achievements for the world.

To become a professional youth worker in the public sector you will need to gain a degree but you may also want to consider gaining a professional youth work qualification from the Joint Negotiating Committee. In each of the four nations the process is slightly different, so we suggest that you contact the relevant organisation:

- In England – the National Youth Agency (NYA) (www.nya.org).
- In Wales – Estyn, which is Her Majesty's Inspectorate for Education and Training (www.estyn.gov.uk/). Courses should be recognised by the Education Training Standards Advisory Committee for Wales.
- In Ireland – courses must be recognised by the North/South Education and Training Standards Committee for Youth Work and you can find more information for Northern Ireland at www.ycni. org/index.htm and the Irish Republic at www.youthworkireland. ie/site/.
- In Scotland – Youth Link Scotland (www.youthlinkscotland.org/). Courses need to be recognised by the Standards Council for Community Learning and Development for Scotland (CLD).

The best way to begin your career in youth work is to start by volunteering. You could contact your local authority as well as charities to explore the possibilities of giving a few hours a week to help them with their youth projects as this will give you a better understanding of the work.

Other professions

In this section we have briefly identified and discussed some of the main professionals who work with young people. These professionals tend to work specifically with this age group. However, there are other people who work with young people but in a more general way such as health professionals, that is, doctors and nurses, social housing professionals and community development workers. It may be that you would like to work with young people but only as part of your client group. Unfortunately, we do not have the space to address all these careers here, but there are other books in this short guide series that do. If you are interested in them then we suggest that you read the recommended texts at the end of this chapter.

Reflective activity

Try to visualise a classroom – it may be one that you sat in while at school, one from a television show such as *The Simpsons* or just a generic classroom that you picture. Is there just one adult in the classroom or are there others? What are they doing there? What is their job role?

Now try to visualise beyond the classroom. Think about the halls, offices and other areas of the school. What different types of classrooms and teachers are there? Some may be teaching indoors, teaching mathematics or science for example, while others might be outside, teaching sports or alternative education for instance.

Thinking about formal education, which is usually what comes into people's minds when you ask them to think about a 'teacher', think about the school in which your classroom was based. Is there a part of the school in which an alternative education is provided? What happens in the building after school? Are there after-school activities, adult education classes or youth clubs? Think about the school holidays – are there holiday schemes or community events that are run there?

Beyond the school that you have imagined, is this the only school in the area? Is there another school, perhaps for young people with special educational needs to attend? Are there other schools in the district? These may be preschools, primary and secondary schools, sixth form and further education colleges. Above this level, in the local city for example, there may also be a university, also known as a higher educational institution.

Many of the people in these varied spaces in these dynamic settings will be teachers and need a professional qualification called a PGCE to do the job. Most of the other people working in the schools, sometimes directly alongside teachers but often in co-operation with them, will be working in one of the professions that we have discussed in this chapter. Some will need a professional qualification to do their work and some will be taking courses offered by their employers. Some of these people will be paid and others will be volunteers.

Finally, without trying to rationalise it, is there a particular space, time or setting that you are drawn to? Maybe this is the area of work that you should be considering in the future? Try to identify what exactly it is about this type of work that you are drawn to? Can you now start to work out how you might work towards a career in that area?

Issues faced by young people

There are particular issues faced by young people that are specific to their developmental stage and can be linked to key transitional ages. These include:

- an increasing number of young people unable to find work and a rise in university fees;
- difficulties in getting on the housing ladder, with a decreasing number of social housing properties;
- being too old for 'children's services', while not having their needs met through 'adult services';
- specific **ageism**.

There are many issues that young people face. These sometimes affect them in the same way as the rest of the population, are sometimes specific to young people but more often than not are issues that people generally face but that create specific issues for young people. Some of these broader issues include those around health where there is a need for provision that is particularly targeted at young people to minimise the issue raised previously where young people fall between the 'child' and 'adult' services gap. This has been an issue for many years, but one that health professionals appear to be taking seriously and actively starting to address. Some of the initiatives being developed in health include youth workers and playworkers (as seen in Chapter Seven) being employed by hospitals to engage and interact with young patients and dedicated youth areas, for the delivery of chemotherapy for example.

As we have tried to impress upon you throughout this book, each and every child or young person is an individual. While they may face many of the same issues and we are able to draw some broad comparisons across life stages and occurrences, no two young people will necessarily react or respond to the same situation, even given that they come from similar backgrounds and experiences, in the same way. As such, adults who work with children and young people utilise broad models and theories to draw on and inform their work to try to support young people to identify and explore their individual needs, hopes and aspirations. One such model is Maslow's (1943) 'hierarchy of needs' (see Figure 8.1).

Figure 8.1: Maslow's hierarchy of needs (original five-stage model)

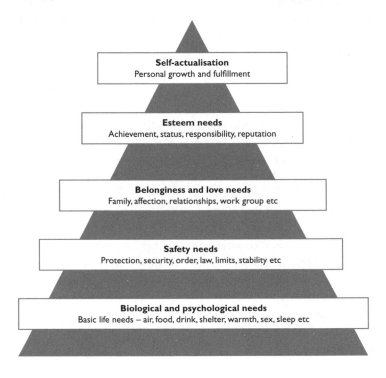

Source: Adapted from Maslow (1943), cited in Chapman (2001–4)

Maslow's model is based on his notion that we are all motivated by need. He proposed that many of the issues people face in their lives are caused by the problems they face meeting those needs. Looking at the model, we can see that it is shaped as a pyramid. Just like models based on a staircase or ladder, there is a suggestion that one should aim to move from the bottom to the top. However, as with staircases you can go up and down, so it is by no means a static or one-way process.

Maslow developed a 'hierarchy' of needs, that is, he arranged needs in the order that he thought was the most important. We can see this from the fact that at the first stage he identified our basic 'life needs', which are, among others, to eat and breathe. At the second stage, Maslow suggested that we need to be safe before we can move on to the third stage and so on. The notion of self-actualisation is a complex one and while it appears to be the goal within Maslow's hierarchy, if you were to achieve this level, it is unlikely that you would maintain it.

If you think about your own life and your needs and priorities, it may be that you feel 'fulfilled' in terms of your personal relationships with your family or partner but do not feel safe in your working environment and thus are not having your needs met in this part of your life. Thus, you can see that the model is not as simplistic nor as one-dimensional as it might first appear.

It is important to understand children and young people's needs as this may be the motivation for their behaviour both positively and negatively. A good example of this with regard to projects provided for children and young people is the breakfast club. There are many examples across the UK of schools and projects providing breakfast. This is because a need has been identified locally that may be caused, for example, by poverty or parents leaving early to get to work. Without a good breakfast, children and young people cannot concentrate throughout their school day, they will find it difficult to focus and in our experience their behaviour deteriorates on many fronts as a result. These projects consistently prove that by ensuring children and young people start the day, and indeed their lives, by meeting their basic needs they have a much greater chance of moving on to meet their higher-level needs later on.

The future of work with young people

As we have highlighted throughout this book, change is the only constant. When governments change, so to do national policies and objectives; as you are aware, a coalition government, made up of the Conservative Party and the Liberal Democrat Party, came to power in May 2010. While as we were writing this book some of the coalition government's vision for the future of services for young people was still being formed and articulated, we do have some notion of how it is planning to move forward.

Almost immediately after the coalition was formed in May 2010, the government changed much of its language regarding young people's services to move away from the Every Child Matters agenda. The Department for Children, Families and Schools (evidence of the Labour government's commitment to working together) changed to the Department for Education. In October 2010, the Every Child Matters website was archived, although still available, and visitors to the site were informed that 'the content of this site may not reflect Government policy' and were redirected to the Department for Education website. For some months, therefore, on the one hand professionals working with children and young people were uncertain as to which part of the Every Child Matters agenda, something that they had been working with for six years, was still relevant, and on the other hand there was little of the coalition government's vision being explained.

However, on 19 December 2011, the government published *Positive for youth: A new approach to cross-government policy for young people aged 13 to 19* (HM Government, 2011). The following is from the Executive Summary, which introduces the government's vision for young people.

Positive for youth

The Government is passionate about creating a society that is positive for youth. Young people matter. They are important to us now, and to our future, and we need them to flourish.

Positive for Youth is a new approach to cross-Government policy for young people aged 13–19 in England. It brings together all of the Government's policies for this age group, presenting a single vision across the interests of at least nine departments.

It has been produced with young people and youth professionals through extensive collaboration and consultation.

Positive for Youth sets out a shared vision for how all parts of society – including councils, schools, charities, businesses – can work together in partnership to support families and improve outcomes for young people, particularly those who are most disadvantaged or vulnerable.

This means working towards a common goal of young people having a strong sense of belonging, and the supportive relationships, strong ambitions, and good opportunities they need to realise their potential.

Young people must be in the driving seat to inform decisions, shape provision, and inspect quality.

Councils are accountable primarily to local people for how well young people do, and how well their services support them.

The Government will publish annually national measures of young people's positive outcomes, and an audit at the end of 2012 of overall progress towards creating a society which is more positive for youth.

Source: HM Government (2011, p 2)

As we write this book, the government's vision is still being digested and interpreted by those currently working with 13- to 19-year-olds across all the sectors and in the full range of professions. Some of the government's new initiatives, such as the National Citizenship Service (NCS), have been piloted and are now being rolled out nationally. Other aspects of its vision will only be recorded when it publishes its first audit of progress, which it plans to do at the end of 2012. Given that this will be only two and a half years after it came into government, what we do know is that this will be a period of great changes and challenges for those of us working with young people.

As we saw in Chapter Two, 'youth' and 'adolescence' are constructs but there will always be young people aged 11 to 19. They will always be facing a period of transition and will always need people to work with them. Gaining a qualification in one of the above professions does not lock or trap you into working with them in that particular way for the rest of your career, something that we hope you identified in the pen pictures of some of our practitioners. Rather it illustrates your ability to work with young people and opens up a door to the field of working with children, young people and their families. As governments and national agendas change throughout your career, a qualification in one of these areas will provide you with the foundation to develop the skills and experience you need to change and challenge where appropriate.

Summary of key points

In this chapter we started to explore:

- the importance of youth and adolescence, referring back to topics that we discussed in earlier chapters;
- the services provided for young people across the spectrum of formal and informal education as well as the different sectors in which you will find work with young people;
- the main professions who work with this age group, including their roles and know where to look for more in-depth information;
- the issues that young people face and looked at Maslow's (1964) hierarchy of needs as a way of understanding how our needs motivate our behaviour.

FURTHER READING

A book written for a broad audience and therefore very 'readable' and easily accessible. It is a great starting point whether you are actively leading work with young people in any setting such as youth clubs, sports settings or uniformed associations. It will also support you to think about how you can develop leadership skills in young people:

Barnes, P. (2002) *Leadership with young people*, Lyme Regis: Russell House Publishing.

A core text for an Open University module entitled 'Working with Young People', which is part of its BA (Hons) Youth Work qualification. It consists of an accessible collection of chapters for anyone new to this kind of work: Curran, S. and Harrison, R. (eds) (2013) *Working with young people*, London: Sage Publications.

A book written specifically for social workers. It discusses the key professionals who social workers work in partnership with such as youth workers, teachers, legal professionals and health workers. Therefore it would be interesting to anyone involved in working collaboratively: Quinney, A. (2006) *Collaborative social work practice*, Exeter: Learning Matters.

ONLINE RESOURCES

Department for Education (2012) *Young people* [online], www.education.gov.uk/childrenandyoungpeople/youngpeople

Directgov (2011) *Next steps: Helping you get on in work and* life [online], https://nextstep.direct.gov.uk/Pages/home.aspx

Infed (2012) *The Encyclopaedia of Informal Education* [online], www.infed.org/index.htm

9

working with all children and young people

Introduction

This chapter emphasises the importance of working with *all* children and young people. This will inevitably mean working with people with different values and from different backgrounds to your own. 'Unconditional positive regard' is an expression that you came across in Chapter Five, and is one that the authors have always used to inform their work. Developed by Carl Rogers, an influential American psychologist, the term reflects an unconditional acceptance of others.

In this chapter we are going to introduce you to the notion of difference and diversity. We are going to highlight the broad range of needs and cultural and religious perspectives of the diverse group that we refer to as 'children and young people'. We are going to identify some of these specific groups in society. Children and young people within these groups will have particular needs and potentially face **discrimination** and **oppression** as a result.

Throughout this last chapter we are going to prompt you to consider why professionals working with these groups must be aware of the specific and individual perspectives and needs of all children and young people. We shall also ask you to reflect on how professionals can either contribute to or challenge discrimination and oppression through their work.

In our work with children and young people we might rather bluntly say that we sometimes dislike the behaviour exhibited by them, or sometimes we might not agree with the choice that others make. Yet it is important that we respect the individual we are working with. Of course we understand that this can be testing. A child or young person might tell you to 'go away' in no uncertain terms or do the very thing that you have just asked them not to. However, by trying to always consider the person behind the behaviour you may be more able to see why they are acting in this way, what need in themselves they are trying to meet and how to support them to meet that need. This is particularly important if someone you are working with is making a decision or behaving in a way that contradicts your own values.

Why should we work with *all* children and young people?

Children and young people make up approximately two billion of the seven billion people in the world (National Geographic, 2011). They therefore make up a considerable proportion of society.

Children and young people are important to us as a society because they are the future generation who will support us as we get older. They are also one of the most vulnerable social groups just because of their age. As we identified in Chapter One, children and young people already face age-related discrimination.

Some of you reading this may feel that you cannot agree with this statement. If this is the case you may wish to consider some of the contradictions of being a 16-year-old in the UK.

If you are a young person living in England, you can get married without parental consent in Scotland, but have to ask your parent's permission to travel there. You can get a job, but aren't allowed to drive there. You can legally have children, but can only get married with a parent's consent.

These contradictions are just in England and Scotland. As you will see from Table 9.1, these tensions are even more evident when we compare across and between countries globally.

Even from these few examples, we can see that there are potentially very mixed messages being given to children and young people about our expectations of them. As we saw in Chapter Three, notions of childhood and youth are actually constructed by society and this idea is supported by the differing ages young people are deemed able to perform different tasks in different countries.

Across the UK and Europe, the ages at which young people can do particular things have become more comparable in recent years. However, as we can see from Table 9.1, there are examples where across UK nations and US states there are varied expectations. While this may not seem so confusing from an adult perspective, in reality, for young people, it can make the difference in the wages they earn and ultimately the difference between going to prison or not.

However, age is not the only form of discrimination and oppression that children and young people face. They often face multiple oppressions, a phrase coined by Thompson (2006). The predominant voice that is heard in our society is white, non-disabled, working, adult. Anyone who doesn't fit these characteristics is often characterised as 'other', being different and strange.

Identity

As we said in the introduction to this chapter, we are going to discuss the diversity within the social group we refer to as 'children and young people'. We have already divided the chapters of this book into subgroups based on age ranges, but this does not even begin to address the range of cultural and religious perspectives or other

Table 9.1: Age of permission

	UK	France	Germany	Ireland	Other
Work	England and Wales: 14 (part time) Scotland: 13	16	15 (must be in some part-time training)	15 (certain restrictions to 18)	Bangladesh: 0
Get married	18 (16 in Scotland) (without parental consent) 16 (with parental/ guardian consent in England, Wales and Northern Ireland)	18	18	18 (below this age with permission)	New Zealand: 18 16 (with parental/ guardian consent)
Join the armed forces	16 (with parental/ guardian consent)	17 (with parental / guardian consent)	17	17 (although some apprenticeship positions are available at 16)	17 (with parental/ guardian consent)
Have sex	16 (17 in Northern Ireland)	15	14	17	US: 16-18 years depending on the state

	UK	France	Germany	Ireland	Other
Participation age	England and Wales: 18 Scotland: 16	16	18	16	Bangladesh: 10
Vote	18 (although there is a lot of support and debate about a reduction to 16)	18	18 (although 16 for some elections in some states)	18	US: 17 in some states for some types of elections. Generally 18 otherwise.
Buy alcohol	18	18	16 (for wine and beer) 18 (for spirits)	18	Jamaica: no minimum drinking age but you have to be 16 to buy it

Sources: CIA (2011), YouthNet (2011)

concepts of identity as related to race, culture, sex, class, ability and sexual orientation.

Pause for thought and reflection

Take a piece of paper and a pen. Draw a picture of a young person. Take care to try to draw them as realistically as you can, although don't worry if you don't consider art to be your strong point – we are not going to ask you to share your drawing. Some of you might like to picture your young person before you start drawing. How old are they? What colour is their hair? What are they wearing? What's their name?

When you have finished your drawing of a young person, do another drawing of yourself. Try and complete this with the same amount of detail.

When both drawings are completed, compare them. Are both drawings non-disabled? Are both male or both female, or are they of a different gender? How similar in social/cultural make-up is the young person to yourself?

Some of you may have realised where we were going with this activity, given the title of the chapter, and drawn a young person very differently from yourself. If this is the case it is still interesting. It tells you in opposites, how you perceive yourself and perhaps should challenge you to think about how the young person, if real, might feel about working with you as a practitioner.

Notion of self

Many programmes that train professionals such as social workers or youth workers expect students to explore their 'notion of self', as Dominelli (2008, p 9) states: 'self-knowledge is a central component of the repertoire of skills held by a reflective practitioner'. As you read through the rest of this chapter, we suggest that you try to position yourself in relation to the themes addressed. How do you define your identity with regard to age, gender, race, class, ability, sexuality and religion? What are your strengths and weaknesses in relation to working with children and young people both generally and in relation to the themes of this chapter? Do you need further training in any of these areas?

It may be that you feel uncomfortable challenging young people and colleagues or discussing certain issues. Workers who are nearer the age of the group that they are working with sometimes report that they need help to find ways to differentiate themselves as a 'leader'. White workers may not feel sufficiently skilled or knowledgeable to discuss the issue of race and **racism**. Heterosexual workers may regularly ask young people not to use the term 'that's so gay', but don't know how to explore their use of language further. Whatever your previous experience or background, you may well find yourself working with children, young people and families that are different to you. This is where further experience, training and talking through the issues with colleagues, supported by reflective practice, will help you to develop your skills. Our point here is that if you do not consider your notion of self, then you will not be able to identify your areas for development and may embark on a career that is well meaning but ultimately oppressive.

One other way of exploring our values in a more sophisticated way is what Freire (1970) termed 'conscientisation', which has its basis in the word 'conscience'. In that sense it could be said to be consciously considering our practice or to try to become consciously aware of the implicit and embedded values that we hold both personally and professionally, which inform our work with children and young people.

In the previous reflective activity, if you drew a young person more 'like' yourself, it might tell you some interesting things about your assumptions. If you decide to work with children and young people, or indeed already are, you should consider how these assumptions might impact on your practice.

In this chapter we hope that we will be able to support you to start doing this. We don't want you to feel bad about what you aren't doing yet; rather we want you to realise that everyone starts somewhere. By trying to engage with the themes and topics in this chapter, you are showing that you want to learn more about this key area of practice.

So where do the ideals we hold come from?

You may well be forgiven for thinking that the ideals we hold regarding the rights of children and young people are relatively recent. Much of the policy being discussed at present with regard to children and young people is being highlighted by practitioners and has usually been introduced since 1997. And you may be aware of some of the discussions being had by the present government and its advisers on new ways of working with this age group.

In Chapter Two, we identified the historical underpinnings and values that informed policy relating to childhood and youth. Some of these events hint at the values society held at the time. As we move on to consider how our social, structural and personal values can lead to discrimination and oppression, we would like you to consider the model presented in Figure 9.2, which highlights the strategies and structures which allow majority groups to keep control and maintain their power.

The PCS model

Neil Thompson is an author who writes about social work, but much of his work can be related to professionals other than social workers who work with children and young people. Thompson (2006) identifies three levels at which the ideals and values that underpin discrimination and oppression occur, as shown in his PCS model (see Figure 9.1). The first of these is at the personal level (P). This sits at the heart of

Figure 9.1: Thompson's PCS model

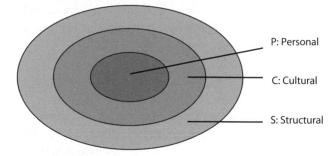

Source: Thompson (2006)

Thompson's model and reflects the personal thoughts, feelings and values of individuals. For those of us who work with children and young people our personal values can stand in the way of non-judgemental practice. Thompson also equates the P in this model to prejudice.

The second level in the model represents the cultural layer (C). In chapter Four we identified how important family and peers are in the lives of children and young people. Our culture and community help us to define what is right and wrong. For those of you currently working with children or young people you may have had reason to challenge them about a perception or value they hold or indeed something they think is a 'fact' that isn't. When exploring where this viewpoint came from you may have ultimately had to make do with the answer that their mother/father/grandfather/friend and so on told them so. This may not feel like the kind of answer that we as adults would find acceptable, but our culture tells young people to listen to adults, so in fact the C at this level can be seen to be self-supporting, with children and young people just doing as they are told. It also reinforces the point that we made in Chapter Four regarding the impact of role models, both positively and negatively.

Finally, the S in the model represents the structures in our society. These structures are created by the policies that we identified in Chapter Two. Other facets of these structures that impact on our values could be the dominant religion in the society in which we live, for example whether the church allows women to be vicars or allows same-sex marriages. National media such as newspapers can also play an important part at this level.

Many of the values held at each level are so part of the world we live in that we do not recognise them. Unless we take part in activities that promote the conscientisation we discussed earlier, you will not be able to truly identify how factors at the structural and cultural levels inform and impact on your own personal values, prejudices and practices. We refer to these moments of realisation as 'Matrix moments'. If you have ever seen the first Matrix movie when, right at the end, Neo finally sees the matrix and realises that the world he 'sees' is actually constructed from code, you will see the comparison to your journey towards greater understanding of the structures and values that are 'sewn in' to all societies. The model presented in Figure 9.2 links some of these 'sewn in' aspects to the strategies and structures that allow majority groups to keep control and maintain their power.

Figure 9.2: Strategies by which majority groups keep control and hold power

Source: Gaine (2010)

Discrimination

Discrimination is a term you may well be aware of. Most people in today's society would identify with the idea that it is wrong to discriminate against people. We tend to discuss discrimination as being all bad. However, we would argue that discrimination is a much more complex notion than that.

First, we discriminate in an appropriate way all the time. That's because to discriminate means to identify a distinction between two things (Thompson, 2006, pp 12-13). So on a given day I might choose to take one route to work rather than another as I know it's half-term so the route will be quicker than the other. Similarly, I might choose to have a low-calorie lunch rather than a sandwich stuffed with cheese as I am on a diet. In both these examples I am discriminating against one choice, but obviously this is different from the kind of discrimination we are talking about in this chapter.

In this chapter the negative forms of discrimination that we are talking about concern the 'different and unequal treatment of individuals, bodies or groups because of perceived differences' (Sapin, 2009, p 212). Such discrimination can be either direct or indirect. If I directly discriminate against you, I treat you differently usually due to your gender, race, ability, culture, religion or age. Indirect discrimination is when a condition, rule or policy disadvantages one group of people more than others. An example of this might be requiring all male staff to be clean-shaven, which would put members of certain religious groups at a disadvantage (Directgov, nd-a).

Prejudice

Prejudice can be explained easily to children and young people by breaking down the word a little. To pre-judge someone or something is to make a decision about them before getting to know them. An example of this is someone pre-judging all young people given what they read about 'young people today' in national newspapers, rather than actually getting to know any of the amazing young people that we have had the honour to work with in our careers. Thompson (2006, p 41) develops this notion even further when he states prejudice is '[a]n opinion or judgment formed without considering the relevant facts or arguments; a biased and intolerant attitude towards particular people or social groups; an opinion or attitude which is rigidly and irrationally maintained even in the face of strong contradictory evidence'.

Anti-discriminatory practice

Anti-discriminatory practice is a way of working that aims to diminish or eradicate discrimination on the grounds of someone's class, gender, age, race/**ethnicity**, sexuality, ability or religion. As such, nti-discriminatory practice is aimed at challenging specific acts of discrimination (Dalrymple and Burke, 2006) against people in the above groups rather than the structures that create oppression.

Before we move on to discuss oppression and anti-oppressive practice it is important to note that some commentators and authors do not draw a distinction between this and anti-discriminatory practice (Thompson, 2006). This is because, as Thompson (2006, p xii) states, 'in (his) view discrimination is the process (or set of processes) which leads to oppression'. As you read the rest of this chapter, you might start to identify your own position on the subject. However, you will need to read much more widely than just this chapter to begin to get a proper understanding of the subject. We have suggested some useful starting points at the end of this chapter.

Oppression

All societies are divided into groups either by choice or by oppressive force. Modern British society is no different from any other in this respect. We might recognise some of these groups as age-related, children, young people, adults and older people or via religion. In modern Britain you can see the kinds of 'groups' we are divided into by looking at the Census or filling out a form that captures the main groups regarding gender, ethnicity, marital status, age and so on.

To be able to competently implement anti-oppressive practice into their workplace, anyone who works with children and young people must make themselves familiar with the diversity within their own community and understand the nature of oppression (Dalrymple and Burke, 1995). Thompson (2006, p 31) defines oppression as: 'Inhuman or degrading treatment of individuals or groups; hardship or injustice brought about by the dominance of one group over another; the negative and demeaning exercise of power.' Thompson's point highlights the fundamental problems that all oppressed groups encounter. These include powerlessness and limited rights, something we can see affects a number of the groups we will discuss later in this chapter but not least of all children and young people with disabilities and asylum seekers.

An aspect that adds another, very complex dimension to features of oppression is the notion of internalised oppression. On a very simplistic level, internalised oppression is the process by which members of an oppressed group begin to believe and advance the negative stereotypes that are promoted about them. For example, young black males may feel that the only choices available to them are to be in gangs as these are the dominant images, examples and role models available to them.

Pause for thought and reflection

Take time to look at a national or local newspaper or search their sites on the internet. What sorts of stories are there about children and young people?

How are they written? What sort of language is used? Are children represented as angels or innocents where teenagers are described as hoodies? Or are you able to find positive stories about children and young people's place and contribution to society?

What message do you think these stories give to children and young people about how society sees them?

Anti-oppressive practice

For Sapin (2009, p 210), **anti-oppressive practice** aims to tackle or respond to 'the effects of oppression through proactive work that raises awareness of prejudice, illuminates different experiences and challenges discriminatory practice of attitudes'. Therefore, anti-oppressive practice is concerned with proactively addressing and challenging the effects of oppression within society (Sapin, 2009). It aims to develop services that respond to people's needs, whatever they are. It is a person-centred approach, which reflects the values of Carl Rogers that we discussed at the beginning of the chapter. It aims both to reduce the impact of wider social oppression on people's lives but also to develop relationships between professionals and those with whom they work, to reduce the impact of the 'power' of the one over the other.

One way in which some professionals, such as play workers, social workers and youth workers, try to reduce the impact of their 'power' over children and young people is to work collaboratively with them. This is something that has been supported by international (United Nations *Conventions on the Rights of the Child*; UN, 1989), European (European Convention on Human Rights; Council of Europe, 1953) and national policy (the Every Child Matters agenda), as we discussed in Chapter Two.

Who are these 'other' children and young people?

In this section we are going to look at groups of children and young people who face discrimination on specific grounds or have particular needs. We will only be briefly highlighting the needs of these groups for you to start to consider how adults who work with children and young people might best engage with them.

Essentially, all oppressed groups are seen as deviant from the 'norm' as they are 'different'. The dominant group in any society such as men, white and non-disabled people define the norm. Notions of normality and deviancy inevitably lead to the maintenance of the dominant viewpoint and the further marginalisation of the oppressed group. Throughout their practice, those who work with children and young people must emphasise to themselves and their group that the oppressed are not responsible for being oppressed. 'Relationships are the backbone of effective ... practice' (Young, 1999, p 5) and it is through these positive and carefully constructed relationships that we can slowly work on these issues with children and young people.

In order to be effective, those who work with children and young people have to accept that oppressions exist so that they are able to work with their groups in a respectful way and meet their needs. Workers also need to recognise that they don't have to be from the oppressed group to work with an oppressed group, but should have knowledge of the oppressions and obstacles that these groups face (Young, 1999). Such an understanding can only be conveyed by or learnt from the groups themselves (Dalrymple and Burke, 1995). This means challenging yourself to find out rather than waiting to be told by the oppressed group what their needs are.

The groups we will be discussing are those who face discrimination based on their:

- class;
- **disability**;
- gender;
- race or ethnicity, including those from Gypsy, Roma and Traveller communities;
- religion;
- sexuality.

Other groups we do not have the space to consider in this chapter, but whom we would like to draw to your attention, are:

- asylum-seeking children and young people (accompanied and unaccompanied);
- those who are NEET;
- those who are the perpetrators or victims of crime;
- young carers;
- those who live in areas of deprivation, including those living in poverty;
- others facing **social exclusion**.

While we will be discussing some of these 'groups' individually, it is important to note that many factors make up one's identity. As such, a child or young person may face discrimination on more than one front or, indeed, someone who you may not perceive to be part of an oppressed group may actually associate themselves with one of these groups.

Class

Your 'class' refers to your social and economic status, so it doesn't exist in 'real' terms. Rather, it is something that our society has created in order to differentiate between people based on their position in society or status. We often hear people refer to lower, middle and upper class, for example, but people's ideas about class have developed and changed over time.

It has been argued that there is more chance for people to move between classes – social mobility – in the UK since the early 21st century. However, the other side to this argument is that things only *appear* to have changed, or that the lower or 'working' classes are being told this in order to placate them. If we look at the coalition government, we can see that 59% of the members of its first Cabinet were privately educated (usually a 'sign' of being upper class) and 69% went to either Cambridge or Oxford University (Spector, 2010).

Terms such as 'chav' perpetuate discriminatory values about certain groups. Terms like this have contested routes: this one may mean

'Council House and Violent' or 'Council House Associated Vermin'. It may also come from the Romani word Chavi, meaning 'child'. It is borne from, among other things, classism. Just like racism, the language about one group perpetuates the myth that they are better (white/upper class) than another (black/lower class). This is often supported and perpetuated by those in the 'middle' who side with the dominant group. This may be because they believe what they read about the 'lower' group in the media and see those in power failing to challenge such ill-informed stereotypes but also, as with bullying, it is safer to side with those in power. Consequently, language is a powerful re-enforcement of in**equality**.

Pause for thought and reflection

If you are reading this book, we assume that it is because you care about and are interested in the lives of children and young people.

Think about the media's representation of young people in your country. Is it generally positive or negative? Can you make a generalisation? We are asking you to consider whether, in your own opinion it is fair.

If you were an adult or older person who didn't work with, care for or spend time trying to understand the lives of children and young people, what conclusions might you draw from media representations of them?

In England there has been a culture of referring to young people as 'yobs', 'hoodies' and 'feral'. How do you think that makes society think about young people and how do you think this makes young people feel about society?

Can you relate this to other groups in society?

Disability

The notions that underpin a society's thinking about disability are reflected, as with all the 'isms' and discrimination we address in this chapter, in the language that is used. For example, the term 'disabled', for many, 'dis-ables' or disempowers those whom society labels with this term. Therefore you may hear terms used such as physical or learning impairment. This is not, as some might say, 'political correctness gone mad', but a better attempt to reflect the individual's experience and needs with the language that is used to describe their situation.

As with most aspects of human relationships, it is usually best to ask the individual how they define their condition or characteristic and the type of language they would prefer you use to describe it. As Jane Elliott, the anti-racism activist, suggests, 'I don't have the right to treat others the way *I* want to be treated—I have the *responsibility* to treat others the way *they* want to be treated' (Eppinga, 2008).

One of the main pieces of legislation in the UK which addresses this area of our lives is the Equality Act 2010, which defines a person as having a disability if:

- they have a physical or mental impairment;
- the impairment has a substantial and long-term adverse effect on their ability to perform normal day-to-day activities (Directgov, nd-b).

Therefore, someone who has an impairment that has a significant or longstanding impact on their normal life would be considered to be disabled. Whether we define ourselves as having a disability, like age, is one of the few aspects of our identity that are likely to change. In fact, as we age we are more likely to have a disability and in turn people who have certain impairments may develop age-related disabilities younger (WHO, 2012a).

Many of us may have a traditional viewpoint of someone who has a disability, such as someone in a wheelchair or with some kind of assistance dog. However, there are many disabilities that you will not be able to tell someone has, just by looking at them. The unseen disabilities that children and young people might have include epilepsy, autistic spectrum disorders, dyslexia and dyspraxia, depression, eating disorders or some self-harming behaviour (Disability Discrimination Act 1995).

Models of disability

As we have alluded to above, some approaches to disability and impairments are perceived to disempower the individual concerned, perhaps presenting them as being a problem. There are considered to be three main models or approaches to 'disability': the medical or individual model, the social model and the rights model. The first problematises the person with the disability. There is something wrong with them and they are defined by their disability. An example of this might be where a youth centre does not have a permanent ramp for wheelchair users to access the building. In every instance a young person has to ask to be let in. While the youth staff might be always happy to help, the young person will always have to ask for help and their 'difference' from the others is constantly noted and the individual has to adapt to their environment.

The social model has been developed in direct response to the issues inherent in the medical model. In the social model, disability is constructed by society rather than being the 'fault' of the individual. Looking again at the example given above, the young person is only disabled by a youth centre with no ramp. If a centre has a permanent access ramp and electric doors, then the young person can move around independently along with their peers.

A third model has been presented in response to identified limitations of the social model (Adams, 2010). An approach informed by the rights model identifies individuals' ability to be independent. 'It shifts the emphasis from the individual and social factors ... to the need for policy and legal measures which advocate and support disabled people's rights and entitlements' (Adams, 2010, p 176).

Gender

Gender is split in to three: male, female and transgendered. The last of these groups, transgendered, are often spoken about in terms of the lesbian, gay and bisexual (LGB) community, thus making it LGBT. However, we hope that you can see this is problematic. The term 'gender' is often used interchangeably with the word 'sex', but they do in fact mean different things (Gaine, 2010), gender being the socially constructed roles assigned to a group and sex being a physical or biological characteristic. Your sexuality is defined by who you are physically attracted to. 'To put it another way: "Male" and "female" are sex categories, while "masculine" and "feminine" are gender categories' (WHO, 2012b).

In Chapter Four we discussed identity formation and in Chapter Six we highlighted the idea of nature or nurture having an impacting on how someone develops and grows as a person. In terms of gender, society creates norms and expectations, such as putting girls in pink clothes and boys in blue clothes as babies. It also creates certain expectations of life choices, for example expecting women to be the main caregiver or stay-at-home parent. As we saw in relation to class, the coalition government's first Cabinet was only 20% female despite women making up 52% of the population. In spite of the Equality Act 2010, there is still obvious inequality in the highest ranks of our society.

You may feel that you cannot affect who sits in our Cabinet, and to some extent you may be right. However, you can affect the work that you do with young people. In accordance with our previous discussions regarding reflecting on your notion of self, you should reflect on and consider what you think about the different genders and what your expectations are of and for young men and women. What do you do in your work to promote positive images of young men and women, from all faiths, races, abilities and classes? How can you work with young men and women to support them to identify their own perspectives on gender and to challenge any stereotypes that they may have?

Race and ethnicity

The term 'race' is often used to define and describe people with different skin colours. It is a contested term, which means that there are a number of different debates that you should explore further in addition to the basic definitions presented here. Once again, the language that we use needs to be thought through. Depending on your age, at some point in time you may have heard or used language such as 'coloured people' to refer to black people. Language creates a narrative that supports the dominant members of society and promotes and supports discrimination and oppression at every level, highlighted by Thompson's (1996) PCS model. In fact, one of the perspectives on 'race' is that it is a term used to differentiate people with different physical characteristics such as skin colour, but does not relate in any way to any genuine biological or genetic differences between people/s (Smith, 2011). We should also note that there is actually only one 'race', Homo Sapiens, or the human race.

Often, you will hear people refer to race in relation to someone's ethnicity. However, there are important differences. A person's ethnicity is 'defined' by belonging to a cultural group. As Smith (2011) states:

> In current usage, 'ethnicity' tends to be used to define individuals who consider themselves, or are considered by others, to share common characteristics which differentiate them from other collectivities or groupings in a society within which they develop distinct cultural behaviour ... the word related to nations or 'peoples' who were not Christian or Jewish, and can be seen as a way of labelling a group both as being different or 'other', and of a lesser order or status.

While the UK population is, according to the 2001 Census, predominantly White British (86%), it is important to remember that we live in a diverse society that is made up of people from a range of different ethnic groups, who may choose not to declare their ethnicity on official data such as the Census. Cultural diversity is something many of us in Britain today are very proud of. However, if you are one of the 86% and are in favour of a multicultural Britain, you may have little or no idea about what it is like being someone from the **black and minority ethnic** community. You will also not know what it is like to grow up in a country where you are a minority, for example one of the 2% of Indians in the UK or even one of the 5% of people who are white but not British.

Gypsy, Roma and Traveller communities

One particular 'group' of people we would like to briefly highlight to you are those from Gypsy, Roma and Traveller communities. While these groups are often referred to together in the way we have above, they are not one homogenous group. The term 'Traveller' has historically been used as a generic term to refer to Gypsies, Travellers of Irish Heritage, Roma, New Travellers, Fairground/Circus families and Boat People. Although this term describes groups of people that have a nomadic lifestyle it does not affirm their separate ethnic identities, which is important (Lander, 2012).

Defining a Gypsy, Roma or Traveller is a matter of self-ascription and does not exclude those who live in houses. Ethnic identity is not lost when members of these groups settle; instead it continues and adapts to new circumstances. Many Travellers today live in a mixture of trailers, mobile homes and permanent housing (D'Arcy, 2011).

People from the settled community often have a stereotypical and prejudiced view of Gypsy, Roma and Traveller communities. Despite Gypsy/Roma and Irish Travellers being explicitly identified in the Race Relations Amendment Act 2000, their experience of discrimination in modern-day Britain has been likened to that 'of black people living in the American Deep South in the 1950s' (Friends, Families and Travellers, nd). Spencer (2005), in her article entitled 'Gypsies and Travellers: Britain's forgotten minority', highlighted the discrimination faced by these groups:

> Overt discrimination remains a common experience. There is a constant struggle to secure the bare necessities, exacerbated by the inability of many adults to read and write, by the reluctance of local officials to visit sites, and by the isolation of these communities from the support of local residents. But we know that these are communities experiencing severe disadvantage. Infant mortality is twice the national average and life expectancy at least 10 years less than that of others in their generation. (Friends, Families and Travellers, nd)

As adults who work with children and young people it is our responsibility to challenge prejudice, stereotyping and discrimination towards all members of Travelling communities, which may include our own assumptions and beliefs.

Religion

Whether you are religious or not, and how you choose to define this is up to you, religion has played a huge part in the development of social norms worldwide. Current debates tend to highlight the differences between traditionally Christian Western countries and Muslims from Eastern countries. However, throughout history religion has impacted on international relations and national laws.

Our religious practices are embedded in our cultural practices. As such, there is an inherent link to a person's ethnicity. This blurring of boundaries is reflected by the UK government's guidance on religious hate crimes:

> Religious hate crimes happen when someone is attacked or threatened because of their religion or their beliefs. Although racial and religious hatred may seem very similar, the police and the courts may treat racial

crimes differently to religious ones. Religious hate crime is not currently recognised as a criminal offence in the same way as racial and homophobic crime. However, if a crime is committed against someone because of their religion, it may be interpreted as an attack on their race as well. This means it can be treated as a racially aggravated or motivated attack. For example, criminal courts have decided that attacks on Sikhs and Jewish people are racial incidents. (Directgov, nd-c)

According to the 2011 Census, 72% of the UK population identify themselves as being Christian. The next biggest religious group are Muslims although only 3% of the UK population identify themselves as Muslim. The other religious groups include Hindus (1%), Sikhs (1%), Jews (0.5%) and Buddhists (0.3%). The second biggest group of people in the UK consider themselves to not be affiliated to any religion (16%).

LGBT (lesbian, gay, bisexual and transgender)

Lesbian, gay, bisexual and transgender people are often referred to as the LGBT community and sometimes as LGBTQ, which can refer to queer or questioning. As you can see, this is a broad and diverse group of people and while these groups may come together at awareness-raising and lobbying activities, it is important to note that each of these groups have differing points of view and experiences. However, one thing that they do have in common is living in a 'heterosexist' society.

Heterosexism is the perspective that assumes that everyone is heterosexual. An example of this is an adult who automatically assumes that a young man will be attracted to young women and so jokes with him about not having a girlfriend yet.

Some adults who work with children and young people find considering LGBT issues very challenging. They argue that children and young people are too young to know whether or not they are gay. The authors' particularly like the response of one young person to a comment like this: 'Why? How old were you when you knew that you were straight?' Another viewpoint that adults can have is to believe that young people can only know that they are LGB once they are sexually active. However, again the authors of this book would challenge such a view by questioning whether this is something we would expect of heterosexual young people.

It may also be that children and young people are aware of LGBT issues because they have parents or siblings who are from one of these groups. Modern families have come a long way from the mother, father and 2.4 children stereotype. As we have tried to reiterate throughout this chapter, adults who work with children and young people need to be aware of how society changes, constantly being conscious of their own stereotypes and assumptions and challenging them in themselves and in others.

Implications for practice

In this section we are going to introduce you to some of the specific practice issues that need to be addressed in order to foster an inclusive culture within an organisation. We will be challenging you to consider the impact of putting policies into practice. We have referred to Thompson's PCS model already so we would like to discuss the Anti-Defamation League's (2003) 'pyramid of hate' (see Figure 9.3) and encourage you to consider the impact of your own and other professionals' personal values and beliefs on the culture and practices within your work setting.

The 'pyramid of hate' is a visual representation of how prejudice can escalate. It is often used to explore and examine the events of the Second World War. The escalation of the scapegoating of Jewish people, which led to the eventual genocide of approximately six million Jews together with Roma Gypsies, people with disabilities and homosexuals, can be observed in the pyramid.

We are sure that we can all think of an example where someone's insensitive remarks or silly joke caused upset. In their defence the culprit says, 'it was only a joke' – a response that we are generally

Figure 9.3: Anti-Defamation League's pyramid of hate

Source: Anti-Defamation League (2003)

socially conditioned to accept. Even if we feel strongly or are quite offended by the comment, to keep challenging it would be seen to be a 'bad sport' or a 'kill-joy'. However, more often than not it allows the individual to make similar remarks in the future as there has been no meaningful discussion as to why they shouldn't. Over time, this can also make the environment in which these comments were made become accepting or tolerant of the viewpoints that can underpin them. While we are not saying that these 'acts of subtle bias' will always escalate to the level of 'genocide', we are saying that they can signify an intolerance and lack of understanding towards a certain group. As someone who works with children and young people, you are uniquely able to discuss and explore their feelings towards and knowledge about such groups and potentially prevent the acts of subtle bias from escalating further. Whatever your role and whether it be in a formal or informal setting, we believe that there is space to discuss these issues with children and young people. It is important that oppressive comments are challenged, maybe not in the moment but these can be revisited through various 'lenses'. In a formal setting this could be in a geography, history or personal, social and health education (PSHE) class in a school or through revisiting the topic when you next meet the young person while doing detached youth work.

Pause for thought and reflection

We the authors believe that failing to challenge young people's use of the term 'that's so gay', to mean something is bad or broken, represents an act of subtle bias.

Do you agree with us? If so, why? If not, why not? Can you substantiate your own views, using something that you have read either in this book or elsewhere to support them?

How can this help when working with children and young people?

So far in this chapter we have looked at some of the main issues and focused on the values and practice of adults who work with children and young people. These ideas and models may help you to build an idea of why people act in specific ways or say certain things. It can also give you a framework for challenging prejudice and discrimination among young people by understanding more fully the structures that underpin and support these views. It reminds us that society enforces our beliefs and helps us to understand how something can become a 'norm' and how best we can go about understanding, explaining and challenging oppression.

It is vitally important that adults who work with children and young people, whether that be in a school, play project, nursery or street-based project, create a conducive learning environment. This is a safe place where children and young people feel comfortable and confident that they will be free from attack, abuse, discrimination or oppression of any kind. It may also be an environment where they are able to hold differing views and religious beliefs and discuss, explore and debate these and be respected. Somewhere where they can talk through their fears and explore what they have been told without fear of being shouted down or ridiculed, or that they will be told that their parents/grandparents/loved ones are wrong.

As we saw in Chapter Two, 'policy' as a term really means to describe 'the way we do things'. A formal policy, such as an organisation's safeguarding policy, explains to employees the way they should act in a given situation to safeguard the young people they work with. Informal policies, ways of behaving or 'norms' can be seen in most teams and organisations, for example if someone makes a cup of tea, are they expected to offer to make other people one? The informal policies tend to be more noticeable when you first join a team or organisation. Over time you become used to them and may no longer be as aware of them – they become natural. This is fine when it is something as innocuous as making a cup of tea, but can become dangerous when it is something as powerful as use of language.

Pen picture – Olivia

Olivia had started to work with a small multidisciplinary team as part of her university studies. On her first day she noticed that her new colleagues were referring to the young people as 'kids' and would openly talk and joke about some of the children and young people they worked with. Keen to fit in, she started to use the same language as them and was eager to join in with their discussions. It was only when she behaved in the same way with her university colleagues that they challenged her. She realised that she had been so focused on fitting in that she hadn't taken a step back to consider whether the team's practice was something she wanted to fit in with.

Olivia's is a common experience for people new to this kind of work. By entering into a 'professional' team, Olivia assumed that her new colleagues would be good role models, but they had fallen into poor working practices. She had been so interested in doing well and being accepted that she had accepted the policies, influences and structures of the team without considering whether they were good practice. As we work with children and young people we must remain vigilant of both our own work practices and those of others to ensure that we monitor our practice and values.

Pause for thought and reflection

What are your thoughts on oppression and discrimination with regard to ageism, disability, classism, racism, religion, and sexuality?

Is there anything that you have read here that has challenged you to think differently or has made you feel uncomfortable?

What could you do next as a result of what you have read in this chapter?

All professionals who work with children and young people need to understand their roles and responsibilities in challenging and minimising discrimination and oppression. These duties may be placed on you by your organisation and national legislation such as the Equality Act 2010. As we challenged you to consider at the beginning of this chapter, it is important that everyone working with children and young people develop their understanding of all forms of oppression. Exploring your own identity will begin to enable this process. Just as with other forms of safeguarding, you should always remember that just as you should maintain vigilance regarding your own practice, you are also responsible for creating an environment where *all* children and young people are cherished and enabled to thrive. This means creating an environment where co-workers monitor and challenge each other and keep up to date with best practice and changing perspectives on all areas of their work.

We have referred to the work of Thompson (2006) and Dominelli (2008) in this chapter and would strongly recommend their books as your next steps. However, should you wish to work with children and young people we hope that the themes within this chapter have inspired you to develop your understanding of discrimination and oppression further. There are a great number of training opportunities available to professionals at local and national levels. There are also many online resources available to you, which we have outlined below. The important thing is to take your time to learn more about the experience of everyone in our society.

SUMMARY OF KEY POINTS

In this chapter, we have introduced:

- the importance of working with *all* children and young people;
- the ideas that underpin discrimination and oppression, including anti-discriminatory practice and anti-oppressive practice;
- the need for adults to be aware of their own notion of self from the perspective that if they are not part of the solution they may be part of the problem.

Finally, we have highlighted:

- the importance of anti-discriminatory practice and the duties we all hold in order to work towards a fairer society where all children and young people are included.

FURTHER READING

A book that introduces readers to important factors regarding working with diversity. It is aimed as Youth and Community Work students and new practitioners, so we feel it would be a good next step for you: Soni, S. (2011) *Working with diversity in youth and community work*, Exeter: Learning Matters.

Similar to the above book, this book is aimed at students and new practitioners, but in the field of social work practice. It develops ideas that we have only begun to introduce you to here: Gaine, C. (ed) (2010) *Equality and diversity in social work practice*, Exeter: Learning Matters.

The first part of this book addresses the ethical context of youth work, which may be too narrow a field for some of you. However, Part 2 discusses ethical issues in practice. We think that the issues identified here are applicable to anyone working in the field: Banks, S. (ed) (2002) *Ethical issues in youth work* (2nd edn), London: Routledge.

ONLINE RESOURCES

Amnesty International (2011) *Children and human rights* [online], www. amnesty.org/en/children

Elliot, J. (2006) *Jane Elliott's blue eyes/brown eyes exercise* [online], www. janeelliott.com/index.htm

UNICEF (2011) *Convention on the Rights of the Child* [online], www. unicef.org/crc/index_30160.html

10

conclusion

In this conclusion we are going to very briefly sum up the main points of each of our chapters in this book. Before we start to do this, we would like to invite you to reflect on where you started at the beginning of the book and reconsider your answers from one of the first activities we suggested that you do.

Pause for thought and reflection

Please reconsider the following questions. We suggest that you jot down your answers before referring back to what you wrote when you started this book.

Why do you want to work with children and/or young people?

Which age group do you think you would like to work with?

What professionals are you now aware of who work with children and young people?

Are any of these professions of interest to you as a future profession? If so, why? Has that changed from before you read this book?

What experience do you already have of working with children and young people?

What experience do you now need in order to achieve the career you would like?

As you have learnt about working with children and young people through reading this book, and perhaps wider research or discussion with practitioners, we wonder whether your answers to these questions have changed. As we said at the beginning of this book, if they have, this is fine! Not only is being adaptable and open an important skill for those who work with children and young people, but you can also now hopefully see how reading this book and researching more widely have impacted on and informed your views.

The first thing that you may have noticed about this book is that we divided it into two parts, the first related to 'preparing to work with children and young people' and the second to 'working with children and young people'. The other way of looking at this division is that the first part discusses the theory and policy of our work whereas the second part identifies practice issues. Of course, this is an artificial separation as theory, policy and practice should go hand in hand. An example of this is the notion of reflective practice, which we introduced you to in Chapter One.

Part One

We have provided you with various opportunities to reflect on and challenge yourself with regard to the topics we have discussed throughout this book. If you have participated in these activities, we hope that you found it a useful process. You will see that there are a number of texts, usually ones that relate to practice, which use similar activities. By participating in them you will get much more from your reading. These activities will also prepare you for any study that you undertake in the future as you will participate in similar activities in the classroom or online. We have also introduced you, in Chapter One, to the idea of reflective or learning journals, something that we hope that you will use to support yourself to develop your understanding of work with children and young people. Hopefully, you also found this chapter useful in 'setting the scene' in which work with children and young people happens.

In Chapter Two we acknowledged and explored the important links between policy and practice, identifying some of the main international and national policies that relate to children and young people, particularly with regard to their rights. We also considered how policies in the UK have developed over time and made note of the very swift introduction of policy into the field from 1997. Finally, we explored how the change in policies had directly informed changes in the working practices of all professionals who work with children and young people.

In Chapter Three we started to explore the social construction of childhood and youth, including considering two different perspectives. The first of these was the universal perspective of the biological or physical reality of childhood and puberty. The second was the social and cultural construction of childhood and youth, which we looked at from both an historical perspective but also a geographical one. From this second perspective we can infer that children in different countries and cultures also have different realities of childhood.

Child and adolescent development were explored in Chapter Four. This chapter introduced the idea of child development theory. You were introduced to Piaget's work on cognitive development and Vygotsky's development of these ideas with regard to the inclusion of social learning and his view that children can learn more if they have help from adults or others who know more than them, that is, the zone of proximal development. We also explored the behaviourist perspective that children learn through cause and effect. The most well-known example of this is Pavlov's dogs.

In this chapter we also explored Skinner's notion of operant conditioning: that if you reward behaviour it will happen again and if you punish behaviour it will act as a deterrent for this behaviour. In this chapter you were also introduced to the work of Erikson, who developed the psychosocial development theory, and Bowlby, whose attachment theory regarding the importance of forming secure attachments during infancy is well known.

Finally we introduced you to a fundamental principle, which we would like you to remember in relation to everything you have read about in this book. This is, that all theories have aspects that are good and positive about them but also that they are all open to some criticism.

Part Two

The first chapter of Part Two of this book (Chapter Five) identified the key practice skills needed to work effectively with children and young people. These skills are the ability to act with professionalism, by understanding the difference between personal values and professional ethics, the importance of personal and professional boundaries and being a reflective practitioner. This means planning your work, managing your time and using professional supervision to support you in these processes. The ability to professionally connect with children and young people, including through verbal and non-verbal communication using a person-centred approach that includes active listening, listener orientation and reflective techniques, was also addressed. Finally, the crucial skill of safeguarding and protecting children and young people through listening, observation and the ability to effectively and sensitively handle disclosures was explored. We also explored the importance of collaborative working and appropriate information sharing as part of the safeguarding process.

In Chapter Six we introduced you to the idea of a curriculum that starts from birth, which is known as the Early Years Foundation Stage. We identified the importance of the early years as a life stage and the range of practitioners who work with children during early childhood, including childminders, workers in children's centres, preschools, playgroups and nurseries, and nannies. Finally, we looked at the issues that are faced by children during this life stage and the future of work with children during early childhood by introducing you to the Tickell Teview.

In Chapter Seven we introduced you to the importance of and explored work with children in their middle childhood. We explored the practitioners who work with children. This included those who are employed as au pairs and within extended schools and the importance of playwork as a profession. We identified the variety of parent practitioner roles, with a specific focus on parent support advisers, and as with the previous chapter we identified some of the issues faced by children at this stage in their lives. Finally, we discussed the Big Society and volunteering as service provision for children and their families.

In Chapter Eight we started to explore work with young people aged 11 to 19. We referred back to topics that we discussed in earlier chapters by identifying the importance of youth and adolescence. We framed the services provided for young people in the spectrum of formal and informal education. We identified some of the main professions who work with this age group, including their roles, and gave you some information regarding where to look for more in-depth information. Finally, we identified some of the issues that young people face and looked at Maslow's (1964) hierarchy of needs as a way of understanding how our needs motivate our behaviour.

In Chapter Nine we identified why *all* children and young people matter. We acknowledged the importance of working with all children and young people as well as how anti-discriminatory practice and anti-oppressive practice are used by practitioners to mitigate and challenge discrimination and oppression. We also explored the need for practitioners to be aware of their own notion of self from the perspective that if they are not part of the solution they may be part of the problem. Finally, we have looked at the implications for practice of these ideals.

Conclusion

We think that one of the most important aspects of a reflective cycle is the 'where next' or 'action' part. This is probably because in our experience it often gets forgotten. We would now like to prompt you to think about 'where next'.

Pause for thought and reflection

Throughout this book, probably ad nauseam, we have reminded you that this is a 'short' guide to working with children and young people. We have also highlighted what a big subject this is and that we are only attempting to start to make you aware of some of the key themes and factors that practitioners working in this field need to consider. Given this, we would ask you to reflect on the following questions:

Were there any parts of this book that you particularly enjoyed?

Were there any parts of this book that you found particularly challenging?

What key messages have you got from reading this book?

What do you need to do to develop your understanding?

If you could only do one thing as a result of reading this book, what might that be?

We would like to conclude this book by reiterating the points that we made in our opening chapter:

- Working with children and young people is a privilege, not a right.
- Children and young people need you to be their youth worker, teacher or social worker and so on, *not* to be their friend or parent.

- Except in specialist circumstances, children and young people do not need to be 'saved'; often they are the best people to resolve their own issues.
- You will probably learn more from working with this group than they will, especially at the beginning.
- Working with these groups can be *very* challenging but we have never found any job so rewarding.

Finally, we sincerely hope that you have enjoyed reading this book. Whichever path you choose, we wish you good luck with your future careers and hope that you enjoy them as much as we have ours.

references

Adams, R. (2010) *The short guide to social work*, Bristol: The Policy Press.

Ainsworth, M.D.S. and Bell, S.M. (1970) 'Attachment, exploration, and separation: illustrated by the behavior of one-year-olds in a strange situation', *Child Development*, vol 41, pp 49-67.

Ainsworth, M.D.S., Blehar, M.C., Waters, E. and Wall, S. (1978) *Patterns of attachment: A psychological study of the strange situation,* Hillsdale, NJ: Lawrence Erlbaum Associates.

Alcock, P. (1996) *Social policy in Britain: Themes and issues*, Basingstoke: Macmillan.

Anti-Defamation League (2003) *The pyramid of hate*, Washington, DC: Anti-Defamation League and Survivors of the Shoah Visual History Foundation, www.adl.org/education/courttv/pyramid_of_hate.pdf

Ariès, P. (1962) *Centuries of childhood*, London: Penguin.

Arnett, J.J. (2010) *Adolescence and emerging adulthood* (4th edition), London: Pearson.

Athey, C. (1990) *Extending thought in young children: A Parent–teacher partnership* (2nd edition), London: Paul Chapman.

Ball, D. (2007) 'Risk and the demise of children's play' in Thom, B., Sales, R. and Pearce, J. *Growing up with risk*, Bristol: The Policy Press.

Bandura, A. (1977) *Social learning theory*, Englewood Cliffs, NJ: Prentice-Hall.

Banks, S. (2001) *Ethics and values in social work*, Basingstoke: Palgrave Macmillan.

Becker, H.S. (1963) *Outsiders: Studies in the sociology of deviance*, London: Macmillan.

Beckett, C. and Taylor, H. (2010) *Human growth and development*, London: Sage Publications.

Beckley, P., Elvidge, K. and Hendry, H. (2009) *Implementing the Early Years Foundation Stage: A handbook*, Maidenhead: Open University Press

Bem, S.L. (1981) 'Gender theory: a cognitive account of sex typing', *Psychological Review*, vol 88, no 4, pp 354-64.

Bertram, T. and Pascal, C. (2002) *Early years education: An international perspective* [online], www.inca.org.uk/pdf/early_years.pdf

Beveridge, W. (1942) *Report of the Inter-Departmental Committee on Social Insurance and Allied Services*, London: HMSO.

BIS (Department for Business, Innovation & Skills) (2012) *National Careers Service for England – statement by John Hayes* [online], www.bis.gov.uk/policies/further-education-skills/john-hayes-national-careers-service-for-england

Boud, D., Keogh, K. and Walker, D. (1985) *Reflection: Turning experience into learning*, London: Croom Helm.

Bowlby, J. (1969) *Attachment: Attachment and loss: Vol 1: Loss,* New York, NY: Basic Books.

Cambridge Dictionaries Online (2011) 'Reflect' [online], http://dictionary.cambridge.org/dictionary/british/reflect_3

Chapman, A (2001–4) *Maslow's hierarchy of need* [online], www.businessballs.com/maslow.htm (accessed 12 November 2012).

Chudacoff, H.P. (1989) *How old are you? Age consciousness in American culture*, Princeton, NJ: Princeton University Press.

CIA (Central Intelligence Agency) (2011) *The world factbook* [online], https://www.cia.gov/library/publications/the-world-factbook/fields/2024.html

Council of Europe (1953) *European Convention on Human Rights*, Strasbourg, France: Council of Europe.

Council of Europe (2011) *Don't get confused* [online], www.coe.int/aboutCoe/index.asp?page=nepasconfondre&l=en

Coomaraswamy, R. (2009) 'Root causes of child soldier phenomenon an UN initiatives' [sic], Address delivered at the University of Michigan, US: http://transcurrents.com/tc/2009/03/post_331.html

Corbett, G. (1981) *Barnardo children in Canada*, Peterborough: Woodland Publishing.

Coster, (2007) 'The social construction of childhood', in P. Zwozdiak-Myers (ed) *Childhood and youth studies*, Exeter: Learning Matters.

CWDC (Children's Workforce Development Council) (2011) *Working in early years* [online], www.cwdcouncil.org.uk/early-years/childcare-careers

CYPU (Children and Young People's Unit) (2001) *Learning to listen: Core principles for the involvement of children and young people*, London: CYPU.

D'Arcy, K. (2011) *Early years support for traveller communities*, Runnymede Bulletin, autumn, no 367.

Dalrymple, J. and Burke, B. (2006) *Anti-oppressive practice: Social care and the law*, Maidenhead: McGraw-Hill.

Davies, B. (2009) 'Youth work and the youth service', in J. Wood and J. Hine (eds) *Work with young people*, London: Sage Publications.

DCSF (Department for Children, Schools and Families) (2006, 2010) *Working together to safeguard children: A guide to inter-agency working to safeguard and promote the welfare of children*, London: DCSF.

DCSF (2007) *Aiming high for young people: A ten-year strategy for positive activities*, London: DCSF.

DCSF (2009) *Guidance for safer working practice for adults working with children and young people*, London: DCSF.

De Mause, L. (ed) (1974) *The history of childhood*, London: Souvenir Press.

Dewey, J. (1938) *Experience and education*, New York, NY: Macmillan.

DfE (Department for Education) (2012) 'Raising the participation age (RPA)' [online], www.education.gov.uk/childrenandyoungpeople/youngpeople/participation/rpa/

DfE (2012b) *Statutory framework for the Early Years Foundation Stage: Setting the standards for learning, development and care for children from birth to five years* [online], http://media.education.gov.uk/assets/files/pdf/e/eyfs%20statutory%20framework%20march%202012.pdf

DfES (Department for Education and Skills) (2005a) *Youth matters*, Green Paper, Cm 6629, London: The Stationery Office.

DfES (2005b) *Common core of skills and knowledge for the children's workforce*, London: The Stationery Office.

DfES (2006) *Youth matters: Next steps*, London: The Stationery Office.

DH (Department of Health) (1999, 2006) *Working together to safeguard children: A guide to inter-agency working to safeguard and promote the welfare of children*, London: The Stationery Office.

Directgov (nd-a) *Discrimination in the workplace* [online], www. direct.gov.uk/en/Employment/ResolvingWorkplaceDisputes/ DiscriminationAtWork/DG_10026557

Directgov (nd-b) *Disability and the Equality Act 2010* [online], www.direct.gov.uk/en/DisabledPeople/RightsAndObligations/ DisabilityRights/DG_4001068

Directgov (nd-c) *Religious hate crime* [online], www.direct.gov.uk/en/ YoungPeople/CrimeAndJustice/TypesOfCrime/DG_10027669

Directgov (2011a) *Key facts about the United Kingdom* [online], www. direct.gov.uk/en/Governmentcitizensandrights/LivingintheUK/ DG_10012517

Directgov (2011b) *Local government structure* [online], www. direct.gov.uk/en/Governmentcitizensandrights/UKgovernment/ Localgovernment/DG_073310

Directgov (2011c) *Extended services through schools*, www.direct.gov. uk/en/Parents/Childcare/DG_172212

Directgov (2011d) *Next step: Helping you get on in work and life* [online], https://nextstep.direct.gov.uk/Pages/home.aspx

Directgov (2012a) *National Careers Service* [online] https:// nationalcareersservice.direct.gov.uk

Directgov (2012b) *National Career Service: Playworker* [online], https:// nationalcareersservice.direct.gov.uk/advice/planning/jobprofiles/ Pages/playworker.aspx

Dominelli, L. (2008) *Anti-racist social work* (3rd edn), Basingstoke: Palgrave Macmillan.

Eppinga, J. (2008) 'Divided by gender: an interview with Jane Elliott', *Journal of Hate Studies* [online], http://guweb2.gonzaga.edu/ againsthate/Journal%206/Interview%20Elliott.pdf

Erikson, E.H. (1968) *Identity: Youth and crisis*, New York, NY: Norton.

Every Child Matters (2010) *Children's trusts* [online], www. everychildmatters.gov.uk/aims/childrenstrusts/

Fass, P. and Mason, M.A. (eds) (2000) *Childhood in America*, New York, NY: New York University Press.

Field, F. (2010a) *The welfare state – never ending reform* [online], www. bbc.co.uk/history/british/modern/field_01.shtml

Field, F. (2010b) *The foundation years: Preventing poor children becoming poor adults. The report of the Independent Review on Poverty and Life Chances*, London: HM Government.

Franklin and Eleanor Roosevelt Institute (2001) *Universal Declaration of Human Rights timeline* [online], www.udhr.org/history/timeline.htm

Freire, P. (1970) *Pedagogy of the oppressed*, London: Penguin.

Friends, Families and Travellers (nd) *Racism and discrimination* [online], www.gypsy-traveller.org/your-rights/law/harassment-and-discrimination/

Gaine, C. (ed) (2010) *Equality and diversity in social work practice*, Exeter: Learning Matters.

Giannini, A.J., Bowman, R.K. and Gianni, J.D. (1999) 'Perception of nonverbal facial cues in chronic phencyclidine abusers', *Perceptual and Motor Skills*, vol 89, no 1, pp 72-6.

Gibbs, G. (1988) *Learning by doing: A guide to teaching and learning methods*, Oxford: Further Educational Unit, Oxford Polytechnic.

Hall, G. (1904) *Adolescence: Its psychology and its relation to physiology, anthropology, sociology, sex, crime, religion, and education* (vols 1 and 2), Englewood Cliffs, NJ: Prentice-Hall.

Harrison, R., Benjamin, C., Curran, S. and Hunter, R. (eds) (2007) *Leading work with young people*, London: Sage Publications.

Hine, T. (1999) *The rise and fall of the American teenager*, New York: Perennial.

HM Government (2011) *Positive for youth: Executive summary*, London: The Stationery Office.

HM Treasury (2003) *Every child matters*, Green Paper, Cm 5860, London: The Stationery Office.

HM Treasury and DfES (Department for Education and Skills) (2005) *Support for parents: The best start for children*, Norwich: HMSO, https://www.education.gov.uk/publications/eOrderingDownload/HMT-Support-parents.pdf

Houlbrooke, R. (1984) *The English family, 1450-1700*, New York, NY: Longman.

Hoyle, D. (2008) 'Problematizing Every Child Matters', *the encyclopaedia of informal education* [online], www.infed.org/socialwork/every_child_matters_a_critique.htm

Ingram, G. and Harris, J. (2001) *Delivering good youth work: A working guide to surviving and thriving*, Lyme Regis: Russell House Publishing.

Inhelder, B. and Piaget, J. (1958) *The growth of logical thinking from childhood to adolescence*, New York, NY: Basic Books.

Ipsos Mori and Naim, A. (2011) *Children's wellbeing in UK, Sweden and Spain: The role of inequality and materialism: A qualitative study*, London: Ipsos MORI.

IRIN News (2003) 'Southern Africa: special report: new thinking needed on "AIDS Orphans"' [online], October, http://2fwww.irinnews.org/Report/46988/SOUTHERN-AFRICA-Special-Report-New-thinking-needed-on-AIDS-orphans-Continued

Kadushin, A. (1992) *Supervision in social work* (3rd edn), New York, NY: Columbia University Press.

Kadushin, A. and Harkness, D. (2002) *Supervision in social work* (4th edn), New York, NY: Columbia University Press.

Kapell, A. (2010) *What is a convention and a treaty* [online], Save the Children and Plan International with War Child Holland, http://resourcecentre.savethechildren.se/content/library/documents/what-convention-and-treaty

Kipling, R. (1902) *Just so stories for little children*, London: Macmillan.

Kruger, F. (2001) 'Child soldiers active in 41 countries', Radio Netherlands, 12 June: www.rnw.nl/hotspots/html/childsoldiers010612.html

Lander, V. (2012) 'Coming from a Traveller background: Gypsy, Roma and Traveller children – living on the margins', in G. Knowles and V. Lander (eds) *Diversity, equality and achievement in education*, London: Sage Publications.

Lansdown, G. (2001) *Promoting children's participation in democratic decision-making* [online], Florence: UNICEF Innocenti Insight, www.unicef-irc.org/publications/pdf/insight6.pdf

Lefevre, M. (2010) *Communicating with children and young people: Making a difference*, Bristol: The Policy Press.

Lewin, K. (1951) *Field theory in social science: Selected theoretical papers*, D. Cartwright (ed), New York, NY: Harper & Row.

Lindsay, G., Cullen, M.A., Band, S., Cullen, S., Davis, L. and Davis, H. (2007) *Parent support adviser pilot: First interim report from the evaluation*, Report no DCSF- RW020, London: Department for Children, Schools and Families.

Little, B. (2010) *NAPP parenting workforce analysis*, London: Children's Workforce Development Council and PriceWaterhouseCoopers, www.cwdcouncil.org.uk/assets/0001/0549/SP155-0910_Parenting_Workforce_Analysis.pdf

McGillivray, G. and Davies, H. (2010) 'Developing yourself as a practitioner', in G. Brotherton, H. Davies and G. McGillivray (eds) *Working with children, young people and families*, London: Sage Publications.

Main, M. (1999) 'Epilogue: attachment theory: eighteen points with suggestions for future studies', in J. Cassidy and P.R. Shaver (eds) *Handbook of attachment: Theory, research and clinical applications*, New York, NY: Guilford Press, pp 845-87.

Marsh, B. (2007) *The Scottish Parliament* [online], http://scotparlhistory.stir.ac.uk/index.html

Maynard, T. and Thomas, N. (2009) *An introduction to early childhood studies* (2nd edition), London: Sage Publications.

Ministry of Education (1960) *The youth service in England and Wales* (The Albemarle Report), London: HMSO.

Morris, H. (1925) *Youth in society: The village college: A memorandum on the provision of educational and social facilities for the countryside, with specific reference to Cambridgeshire*, Cambridge: Cambridge University Press.

National Geographic (2011) *7 billion: How your world will change*, App., Washington, DC: National Geographic.

NCMA (National Childminding Association) (2010) *Become a registered childminder* [online], www.ncma.org.uk/childminders.aspx

NCS (National Careers Service) (2012) *Careers Adviser* [online], https://nationalcareersservice.direct.gov.uk/advice/planning/jobprofiles/Pages/careersadviser.aspx (accessed 12 November 2012).

NCVO (National Council for Voluntary Organisations) (2007) *Collaborative working: Partnership between voluntary organisations* [online], www.ncvo-vol.org.uk/collaborativeworking/index.asp?id=2039

Nevid, J.S. (2012) *Psychology: Concepts and applications*, 4th edn, Belmont: Wadsworth.

Newman, T. and Blackburn, S. (2002) *Transitions in the lives of children and young people: Resilience factors*, Edinburgh: Barnardo's Policy, Research and Influencing Unit/Scottish Executive Education Department.

NHS (National Health Service) (2012) *Hospital play staff/registered play specialist*, [online], www.nhscareers.nhs.uk/details/Default.aspx?Id=911

Northall, M. and Smith, C. (nd) *Supporting lone mothers to enter the workplace*, Birmingham: Newman College of Higher Education/European Social Fund, www.newman.ac.uk/courses/SC_PD/esf_reports/Lone%20Mothers%20Report.pdf

NI (Northern Ireland) Direct (2010) *Information and services* [online], www.nidirect.gov.uk/index.htm

NSPCC (2012) *An introduction to child protection legislation in the UK*, Factsheet, London: NSPCC Inform.

Ofsted (2012) *Understanding an early years and childcare inspection report* [online], www.ofsted.gov.uk/early-years-and-childcare/for-parents-and-carers/understanding-early-years-and-childcare-inspection-

Oliver, B. and Pitt, B. (2011) *Working with children, young people and families: A course book for foundation degrees*, Exeter: Learning Matters.

ONS (Office for National Statistics) (2011) *United Kingdom: Local authority districts, counties and unitary authorities* [online], www.statistics.gov.uk/geography/downloads/CTY_LAD_APR_2009_UK_MP.pdf

Parliament UK (nd) *Living heritage: Going to school* [online], www.parliament.uk/about/living-heritage/transformingsociety/livinglearning/school/overview/

Payne, M. (2000) *Teamwork in multiprofessional care*, Basingstoke: Macmillan.

Piaget, J. (2001) *The psychology of intelligence*, London: Routledge.

Play England (2011) *Government to discontinue national play contracts* [online], www.playengland.org.uk/news/2011/02/government-to-discontinue-national-play-contracts.aspx

Pollock, L. (1983) *Forgotten children: Parent–child relations from 1500-1900*, Cambridge: Cambridge University Press.

Postman, N. (1994) *The disappearance of childhood*, New York, NY: Vintage Books.

Raiker, A. (2007) 'Cognitive development' in Zwozdiak-Myers, P. (ed) (2007) *Childhood and youth studies*, Exeter: Learning Matters.

Rhodes, C. (2012) *Youth unemployment statistics* [online], www.parliament.uk/briefing-papers/SN05871

Rogers, C. (1983) *Freedom to learn for the 80s*, Columbus, OH: Charles Merrill.

Sapin, K. (2009) *Essential skills for youth work practice*, London: Sage Publications.

Savage, J. (2007) *Teenage: The creation of youth culture*, New York: Viking.

Scheper Hughes, N. (1992) *Death without weeping: The violence of everyday life in Brazil*, Berkeley, CA: University of California Press.

Scottish Government (2011) *Youth justice* [online], www.scotland.gov.uk/Topics/Justice/crimes/youth-justice

Shorter, E. (1975) *The making of the modern family*, New York, NY: Basic Books.

Skillsactive (2011) *Playwork* [online], www.skillsactive.com/our-sectors/playwork

Skinner, B.F. (1938) *The behavior of organisms*, New York: Appleton-Century-Crofts.

Smith, M.K. (2000, 2004) 'Full-service schooling', *the encyclopaedia of informal education* [online], www.infed.org/schooling/f-serv.htm

Smith, M.K. (2001) 'Ragged schools and the development of youth work and informal education' [online], *the encyclopaedia of informal education*, www.infed.org/youthwork/ragged_schools.htm

Smith, M.K. (2002) 'Youth work: an introduction' [online], *the encyclopaedia of informal education*, www.infed.org/youthwork/b-yw.htm.

Smith, M.K. (2011) '"Race" and difference – developing practice in lifelong learning', *the encyclopaedia of informal education* [online], www.infed.org/lifelonglearning/b-race.htm

Spencer, S. (2005) 'Gypsies and Travellers: Britain's forgotten minority', Friends Families and Travellers (nd) *Racism and Discrimination* [online], www.gypsy-traveller.org/your-rights/law/harassment-and-discrimination/ (accessed 23 July 2012).

Spector, F. (2010) 'Does "new politics" mean more Oxbridge males?', *Channel 4 News* [online], www.channel4.com/news/articles/vote_2010/missing%2bwomen%2band%2bthe%2bpublic%2bschool%2binvasion/3647587.html

Stone, L. (1979) *The family: Sex and marriage in England, 1500-1800*, New York, NY: Harper & Row.

Sylva, K., Melhuish, E.C., Sammons, P., Siraj-Blatchford, I. and Taggart, B. (2004) *The Effective Provision of Pre-School Education (EPPE) Project: Technical paper 12: The final report: Effective pre-school education*, London: Department for Education and Skills/Institute of Education, University of London.

Tameside Metropolitan Borough (2011) *Playgroups and pre-school groups* [online], www.tameside.gov.uk/surestart/childcare/playgoups#Playgroup

The Wall Street Journal (2011) *Europe's debt crisis timeline* [online], http://online.wsj.com/public/resources/documents/info-EZdebt0210.htmlUN

Thom, B., Sales, R. and Pearce, J. (2007) *Growing up with risk*, Bristol: The Policy Press.

Thompson, N. (2006) *Anti-discriminatory practice* (4th edn), Basingstoke: Palgrave Macmillan.

Tickell, C. (2011) *The early years: Foundations for life, health and learning: An independent report on the Early Years Foundation Stage to Her Majesty's Government* [online], http://www.education.gov.uk/tickellreview

UN (United Nations) (nd) *UN at a glance* [online], www.un.org/en/aboutun/index.shtml

UN (1948) *The Universal Declaration of Human Rights* [online], www.un.org/en/documents/udhr/

UN (1989) *Convention on the Rights of the Child*, New York, NY: UN, http://www2.ohchr.org/english/law/crc.htm

UNICEF (United Nations Children's Fund) (2011) *Convention on the Rights of the Child* [online], www.unicef.org/crc/

UNICEF (2012) *About UNICEF: Who we are* [online], www.unicef.org/about/who/index_history.html (accessed 12 November 2012).

UN News Centre (2011) 'As world passes 7 billion milestone, UN urges action to meet key challenges' [online], www.un.org/apps/news/story.asp?NewsID=40257 (accessed 12 November 2012).

Vygotsky, L. (1962) *Thought and language*, New York, NY: Wiley.

Wagg, S. (1992) '"One I made earlier": media, popular culture and the politics of childhood', in D. Strinati and S. Wagg (eds) *Come on down? Popular media culture in post-war Britain*, London: Routledge.

Walker, S. (2003) *Working together for healthy young minds*, Lyme Regis: Russell House Publishing.

Waterhouse, R. (2000) *Lost in care: Summary of report*, London: HMSO.

Wenger, E. (1999) *Communities of practice: Learning, meaning and identity*, Cambridge: Cambridge University Press.

WHO (World Health Organization) (2012a) *Disability and health* [online], www.who.int/mediacentre/factsheets/fs352/en/

WHO (2012b) *Gender, women and health* [online], www.who.int/gender/whatisgender/en/

Williams, R. (2011) 'Charities No Smoking Day and British Heart Foundation to merge', *The Guardian online*, 28 September, www.guardian.co.uk/society/2011/sep/28/charities-no-smoking-day-british-heart-foundation-merge

Young, K. (1999) *The art of youth work*, Lyme Regis: Russell House Publishing.

YouthNet UK (2011) 'What age can I', *The Site* [online], www.thesite.org/homelawandmoney/law/yourrights/whatagecani

Index

Note: The following abbreviations have been used – *f* = figure; *t* = table